GOSPEL Images

GUIDED MEDITATIONS
FROM THE STORIES OF JESUS

JOHN HENSTRIDGE

ABINGDON PRESS
NASHVILLE

GOSPEL IMAGES: GUIDED MEDITATIONS FROM THE STORIES OF JESUS

Text copyright © John Henstridge 2000. Original edition published in English under the title Step *into* the Light *by The Bible Reading Fellowship, Oxford, England. Copyright © The Bible Reading Fellowship 2000.*

Abingdon Press edition published 2002.

ISBN 0-687-09837-8

All Scripture quotations, unless otherwise noted, are taken from the *New Revised Standard Version of the Bible*, copyright 1989, Division of Christian Education of the National Council of the Churches of Christ in the United States of America. Used by permission. All rights reserved.

Susie Ware and Jo Williams have granted permission for use of their song lyrics, recorded in England in a collection called "Down to Earth."

02 03 04 05 06 07 08 09 10 11—10 9 8 7 6 5 4 3 2 1

MANUFACTURED IN THE UNITED STATES OF AMERICA

ACKNOWLEDGMENTS AND DEDICATION

The process of bringing these meditations into a form for people to use was a humbling experience and also a great blessing. It was humbling because no one can do such a work without a great deal of help from God, both directly and through the support and guidance of other people. And this is also the blessing—the blessing of God's generous and loving inspiration and the blessing of the support and help of various marvelous people.

So this collection of meditations is dedicated to all who have shared them at any time and to all who have been wonderful in giving support, encouragement and expertise, without whom this book would have been much impoverished.

The first meditations were written down for my niece, Julia, to use—a response to her need and her courage. She then suggested I should write them into a book. Subsequently the meditations were used, among others, with the congregation of St Augustine's, Aldershot (Sundays in Lent 1993); with those at a Good Friday Three-Hour Service and later at a Quiet Day for a house group (Great Bookham); on an Alpha course at the session on prayer (Elstead, autumn 1997); at a Guildford Diocese clergy study day (December 1998); and with various other groups.

Special thanks to the editor at Bible Reading Fellowship, Naomi Starkey, who has not only been helpful and encouraging, but whose insight showed me how to put the meditations into a usable form. I am very grateful to Susie Hare and Jo Williams for allowing me to use quotations from songs from their collection *Down to Earth*. The Rev. Alan Taylor, Vicar of St. Aidan's, Leeds, has been very helpful in ensuring the accuracy of the geography and nature of the Holy Land—and has enlightened me on the way. A very special "thank you" to Jennifer Rees Larcombe. Not only has Jen been generous in writing the foreword, but she has also been wonderfully encouraging and supportive throughout. I am enormously grateful to my daughter-in-law, Catherine, who has given many hours, and brought her considerable skills to bear, not only on proofreading, grammar, and punctuation, but also on making many invaluable suggestions on the use of language and numerous aspects of the content.

Finally my grateful thanks to my family for their encouragement and especially to my wife, Prue, who has always supported me in my ministry.

To all of these this book is dedicated, and to the greater glory of God.

Any faults are entirely mine, but what is good is a gift from God, and I pass it on to you with a prayer that you may share the gift and grow in his joyous love. To God be all honor and glory.

CONTENTS

FOREWORD

I was definitely *not* enjoying a day in bed with flu when I began to read the manuscript of this book. I was hardly half-way down the first page of the introduction before I was riveted. For years I've been trying to convince the person I was brought up to be that praying is not just a string of words, but being quiet with Jesus and listening to him. I know that in my head, but somehow I still feel vaguely guilty when I "do nothing" in God's presence. I was taught to use every minute of my "Quiet Time" to learn more about the Bible and to help others by interceding for them.

Of course these things are an important part of relating to God and serving him, but the busy, active "Martha" side of my spirituality left no room for the contemplative "Mary" to blossom. The "doing" and the "being" have argued constantly inside me for many years.

Reading John's philosophy of prayer finally banished the last shreds of guilt. It really is OK just to sit with Jesus and listen to him.

I decided I would try one of the meditations, just to see how it worked. I have to confess that I am still astounded by what happened. I've often tried to meditate on one of the stories of Jesus, using my imagination under the guidance of his Holy Spirit, but I've never found concentrating easy. Because John takes us through the meditations so gently and sensitively, I suddenly found I could do it. Like learning to swim or ride a bike, it becomes easy when someone is there with you, to give you confidence.

The story I had chosen was totally familiar to me. I had told it to my own children and to others in Sunday school classes, used it as the basis for many a sermon; and I had read it myself at least a hundred times.

Because of the way John led me through the story, however, the Holy Spirit was able to reveal something about an incident in my past that I had never realized before. I saw the whole situation through the eyes of the four other people who had been involved and suddenly understood why each of them had reacted to it in—what had always seemed to me—such a bewildering fashion. Somehow the Holy Spirit was able to take me "inside" each of them in turn, to feel their pain and experience their reactions to what had happened.

I can still hardly believe the impact that first meditation made upon me; I can only describe it as "life changing."

I cannot recommend this book to you highly enough. For me, it has been a very helpful teaching book on "how to pray," but I know I shall return to these meditations many times over in my own private "appointments" with God because it is also an excellent devotional book. Yet perhaps its greatest value will be as a basis for group meditation. This book is so unusual and so very special that it does not fit into the usual "slots," such as "teaching," "devotional," "group study material." It fits comfortably into all those slots at once, making it worth its weight in gold.

Jennifer Rees Larcombe

INTRODUCTION

Purpose

These meditations are for people who want to step beyond the prayers of the "shopping list" or the "cry for help" kind, and prayer which consists only of words, into prayer which is aimed at building a relationship with Jesus. Many books tell you *how* to pray. Few actually *do* the prayer, leading you through it. This is a collection of meditations for *doing* prayer, prayer which aims to build that relationship, to live in the light of Christ—to "step into the light." These meditations are mainly for groups of people, although they can also be used by individuals.

Meditation in a group (or even a congregation) is particularly powerful. Christians together get a very real sense and experience of the presence of Jesus, who promises to be with us when we meet in his name. Each person is built up, and all are built together; there can be real growth in the spiritual life of each Christian and in the community of Christians together. "As each sing his praise differently, all together form a symphony of love" (Saint John of the Cross).

What Is Prayer?

Prayer is about being with Jesus and learning to listen to him, to know him, to love him, and so become more like him, at one with him. The apostle Paul talks about being "in Christ" and about "Christ living in us." That is the essence of prayer, rather than the endless stream of words we have so often got used to, which tend to block out listening. Prayer is "being" rather than "doing" or "speaking"—although these have their place in the life of prayer. Prayer is a kind of inner life, a sensitive, growing awareness of God. The life of prayer is different for each person; we are all made as individuals by God, who wants us to grow, not into a standard model, all exactly the same, but into the person God has created each of us to be: our unique, true selves. This is ultimate reality, living in the light of Christ.

Prayer should lead to growth. Growing into the person God wants us to be is not something we do; it is what God does in us, given time and opportunity. As one American writer on spirituality, Suzanne Zuercher, puts it: "Genuine conversion is not a task *we* can bring about. If we live our lives fully, we will be tested and tempered by such commitment until we are shaped into the person God intends us to be, rather than the one into which we form ourselves" (*Enneagram Spirituality*, Notre Dame, Ind.: Ave Maria Press, 1992). Prayer is God's lifelong work in us, of making us whole—our conversion.

Prayer starts with learning to know Jesus, and develops through knowing him better and opening up to him more and more. We may ultimately be rewarded with that prayer which needs no words, being with Jesus in silent awareness and contemplation. But for a lot of the time most of us tread a slower path. This means allowing God to use our minds, our thoughts, our imagination, and our hearts to draw us close to God. We need help with this, and a ready form of help is at hand: the Bible. The Bible is where we learn about Jesus, and get to know more about him, because that is where we see his love in his actions and words. We, too, can experience Jesus in action and words. The Bible is not "magic," but God uses the power of his Word, Jesus, to be made known to us through the words of the Bible.

Prayer builds up over time; and through prayer God builds us up. After a while we can look back and see how much progress God has made in us— rather like climbing a hill, and then turning round to be surprised by the view. There are lots of surprises along the way—he is the God of surprises!

How to Lead the Meditations: Notes for Group Leaders

Since these meditations are primarily for use with groups, the following notes are designed to guide those leading the meditations, and enable them to make the most of the opportunity. However, as a leader, you can of course be flexible, and use your experience to develop the most appropriate ways of leading the meditations. If you are using the meditations on your own, there are some notes to help you later in this introduction, but you may find it helpful to read the notes for group leaders first.

The first time only, if appropriate, try to hold an open discussion with the group. Ask them about their experience of prayer, what it means to them. You will not be surprised to discover that many of those who worship regularly in church have virtually no prayer life at all, but you may also be surprised at the depth of experience that others have. Ask people what prayer means to them (if the group is bigger than six or eight this can be done in pairs or threes to make it easier for people to talk on a personal level). Help people to discover how varied prayer can be; and, of course, help people to see that each person's way of prayer is valid and is worth sharing with others. There is a great deal of learning for all of us, leaders included, in this exchange of experience.

When all this has been explored, you may find it worthwhile talking through what the prayer of "being with Jesus" can mean; Anthony de Mello, a great spiritual writer, talks of our being in touch with God through a "spiritual mind" and a "spiritual heart." We can be in touch with God through all our senses, but especially through a spiritual sensitivity. Developing this spiritual sensitivity is an essential part of sharing in these meditations.

Finally, lead the group through the method of prayer in this book which they are going to share: preparation, story, meditation using the imagination (and usually being a character in the event), followed by debriefing and reflection.

People need to know that there is a variety of responses to a guided meditation. Some may feel deeply moved, others not at all. An individual's response may vary from one meditation to another. All responses are valid; people should not be disappointed if they feel moved at one time and not another. Quite a hard lesson for many Christians to learn is that how we *feel* is not that important. We may sometimes be rewarded with all sorts of feelings, but our feelings are a very unreliable guide to our relationship with God. What really matters is that we have opened ourselves to God. His love for us never changes, and he will choose how he uses the time to work in us.

Please note that some people do not have a vivid imagination and may find it difficult to use this gift which God has given us. There is a section later in this introduction which includes an exercise to help people practice using their imagination with familiar material. This is intended to help them learn that they can develop this gift, and work on it. One important aspect of imagining events in the life of Jesus is that people do not actually have to picture him. He can be there, and you can be aware of him without a specific image of him, even though you visualize the scene and feel part of it. Nor do people have to picture Jesus in biblical dress; he could be in modern dress. What matters is whatever helps people to become aware of Jesus as real, as truly alive, now.

You will also need to explain that although the events on which the meditations are based are from the New Testament, the setting of the meditation may be in Palestine in the time of Jesus or it may be in our own time. The setting may also move from one time to the other. Sometimes the meditation will not follow the events of the Bible story very precisely (the reason for this is explained below).

To Use a Meditation

1. Arrange for everyone to be comfortable, but in a position in which they can be alert and focused. For most, this means being seated in a firm chair with space around them, but not too far from their fellow group members. Do avoid soft, easy chairs—being too relaxed and comfortable leads to loss of concentration. Those involved need to have a sense of fellowship with each other. There needs to be an atmosphere of peace and calm, so allow plenty of time to settle down and be still. You may want to use a short prayer for peace and stillness before you begin the account from the Gospels.

2. Tell the "story." The retelling is aimed at "refreshing" the account of the actions in the Bible. Most regular churchgoers are overly familiar with the New Testament events, so we need to find new ways of making them vivid. The most important aspect of telling is that the account needs to feel real—an event of today and not long ago. As you tell it, think of Jesus alive and real and present now.

3. Prepare people—by helping them to achieve a sense of inner stillness, sometimes referred to as "movement into stillness." This preparation is vital for people to come to a sense of inner peace, so it is worth allowing plenty of time to do this. I usually allow quite lengthy silent spaces as people are led into tranquillity and readiness for meditation. I find it helps people to use their breathing as part of this movement into stillness; in particular, try to use the idea of breathing *in* the Holy Spirit and breathing *out* all fear and worry and sin. This is very biblical—Paul reminds us that it is the Spirit who prays in us, and indeed the Old Testament often uses breath as a metaphor for the Spirit—the breath of life.

An example of the way I would help people to prepare for meditation follows below. You need to allow varying times of silence as people move into stillness. You should also vary the preparation for each of the meditations— no two preparation times should be exactly the same. In the example below, allow silence at the end of each line. The length of silence varies; your experience will help you become sensitive to the group's readiness to move forward. In particular, do allow a longer silence when people are learning to breathe slowly, and allow the Holy Spirit to breathe in them. Then, as you sense that people are achieving an inner peace, you can move forward at the appropriate pace, and then into the meditation:

Let's take some time to be still.
Try to sit comfortably, but alert and focused.
Set aside all that is occupying your mind.
Empty your mind of all those worries, problems, concerns.
Be still and calm.
Breathe slowly and deeply.
Take time to breathe.
Focus on breathing in the Holy Spirit,
and breathing out all anxiety and fear and sin.
Let him take over.
Take time. Let him breathe peace into your heart.
Let the peace and calm of Jesus fill your heart and mind.

Next—only when you sense that people are quite ready:

Now let's bring our imagination to work. Try to picture the scene.
Make a picture in your mind's eye—like a television scene.
You are the paralyzed person . . .

Thus you begin the first meditation.

4. Take the group through the meditation. You will need to have used the meditation yourself before leading others through it—using it as *prayer,* and never just reading it. This will help you to gain a sense of the spaces needed for the imagination to work. Your own preparation will also involve some reading through to enable you to pace the words and the silences in order to match the way in which the group is moving forward.

The meditations are set out in short sections. A pause for silence is appropriate at the end of each line break, with a longer pause at the end of each paragraph. Try to use your own imagination and be part of the group meditation as well. This will help you to get the pauses right. The spaces for silence should not be all the same length, but should vary to allow sufficient time for the imagination to work. Your preparation will help you, along with your sensitivity to the way the group is responding.

You do not need to dramatize the meditations; it is important to let Jesus speak to people through the Gospel event and the use of their imagination. On the whole, I have found a fairly calm style to be most appropriate. However, some events are dramatic, such as the storm on the lake; then you can let the drama speak without overdoing it. The meditations are intended to do the work of guiding people for you.

5. Ending the meditation. At the end of each meditation there is a time for stillness and silence. You can allow time for this until you sense the group is ready to go on, and you may then wish to say a very short prayer.

6. Debriefing. It is always important to help people to move from being in the character of the person they have in their imagination, to coming back down to earth. The way to do this is to ask people to report on their experience so that they step outside it. The way in which a particular meditation affects an individual is unpredictable, and may vary enormously from person to person. There should be an opportunity for reflection after debriefing at the end of each meditation (see below) and some notes are given at the end of each meditation.

Sometimes God uses this time to speak to a person; others will have been still and relaxed in God's presence. Some may be disturbed, emotional, frustrated, or even angry for some reason. The group members need to know that *all* responses are acceptable. (Incidentally, a healthy group will have a range of responses, rather than all having the same experience.)

People need help to come to terms with different kinds of reaction, and in particular you need to ensure that those who may be disturbed or angry feel that they are accepted. They may need some help to explore their emotions, but we should be wary of invading privacy. Others may have felt that there was little to experience—little or no sense of Jesus' presence and no new thoughts or feelings on their part. Again, reassurance is important. The time has been given to God, and he will use it to work in each person. Writers on prayer have pointed out the dangers of relying on feelings, which are often simply a subjective reaction, and may do little or nothing for spiritual growth. The time of prayer may seem empty, but God works through it. Often the real growth and the real changes come right outside the prayer time in the events of every day.

7. Reflection. The group can now move on to reflect on their experience, and look at ways in which their thinking, their spirituality and their living may change as a result of the meditation. What impact will their experience have on their everyday life of prayer, work, leisure, and Christian commitment? There are some pointers to introducing the reflection after each meditation. You do not, of course, need to use these, and you may find other creative ways of leading people. In the early stages of a group meeting for meditation, the members may be less willing to discuss their responses to the meditation. Over time they will develop trust in you and one another, and as time goes on you may well be surprised by the responses—especially by the range of responses—which people report.

Normally I close the meeting (certainly in its "formal" sense) with prayer after the time for debriefing and reflection. However, if you are using the meditations with a whole congregation in church, you could simply close with a prayer after the silence at the end of the meditation. Some of Paul's letters have very appropriate verses in them to adapt for prayer, for example, Ephesians 3:14-21.

Using the Imagination

People tend to use one of three ways to think about, and particularly to recall, events: *pictorially*—using pictures, diagrams and so on; *verbally*—using words; *emotionally*—using their feelings. Everybody can use all three ways, but each person tends to use one rather than the others. The use of pictures, the faculty of imagination, is especially valuable in prayer, and is the main gift used in these meditations, although the other gifts are used as well. There may be those who find using their imagination difficult. For this reason I have found it useful at the beginning of a series of meditations (for example, with a congregation during the Sundays in Lent) to start with an exercise, a "practice." On those occasions, I began with a talk about the prayer of meditation, and then we did the exercise described below.

The exercise uses some event in each person's memory, helps them to bring it to life in their imagination, and leads them into prayer. I give an example below which is rather like one of the meditations. After an introduction, we need to become still and reflective to prepare, moving into stillness, before moving into the exercise:

Think of an event in your past, a time when you were happy, relaxed; at peace, enjoying yourself; a time when you felt really good.

It may have been a time with the family, on holiday, with a group of friends, at a party.

Now put a picture in your mind's eye—try to see a picture of the scene, as if you are looking at a mental video.

17

First focus on the setting, try to build the whole background to the scene— the place, the circumstances. What can you see? What sort of place is it? A house? An outdoor setting? A room?

What are the background colors? The sounds? The movements?

Now put all the people into the picture; look at each one in turn, and identify them. Think what each one looks like; what are they wearing? What colors have they got on? Can you see what they are doing? Can you hear what they are saying? What are the expressions on their faces?

Next place yourself in the event; be there yourself, taking part, not just looking on. What you are feeling?

Allow yourself to enjoy the event, the good feeling, the happiness—maybe the fun, the laughter.

Finally, we are going to bring one more person into the scene. Try to imagine that Jesus is there with you. Be aware of his presence. He brings light and joy. He is the source of the light and joy you feel, the happiness, the laughter.

Rest there in that scene for a moment. Enjoy the extra dimension that Jesus brings. Maybe you want to say something to him. Perhaps to thank him. Or just to rest there with him.

After a period of silence, I end the exercise with prayer. This exercise can be repeated—people can think of different events in their lives; and they can do the exercise on their own to work on their imagination. If you do repeat the exercise, the actual wording should be varied—use your own words.

Using the Meditations on Your Own

You can use the meditations on your own, if you wish. You will need a time and a place where you can be quiet and at peace. You may find it helpful to look through the meditation before you use it so that the use of the words does not hinder your imagination, but remember the meditations are not for reading, they are for praying. Before using the meditation, find a way of "moving into stillness." Use a posture that is comfortable, but attentive and focused. Then practice the use of your breathing to move into stillness, breathing in the Holy Spirit, and breathing out all that hinders. When you are ready, begin the meditation.

In each meditation, take plenty of time to build the picture, and move forward slowly as the event unfolds. Avoid the temptation to rush ahead, and allow your imagination to work on the scene, the people, the events. As you come to each line break (see above), pause to picture what is happening, and if you wish, you can explore beyond the words of the meditation.

When you come to the end of the meditation, you may have some response—peace, joy, thankfulness, for example—and if so, then give time to these, savoring the presence of Jesus with you. Different meditations will bring different responses, and the same meditation may bring different responses at different times; sometimes you may have little or no response. All of these are fine. When you are ready, you can reflect on what God is showing you, and turn it into prayer.

One of the values of meditation is that, as you go about the business of the day, thoughts and feelings come back to you. This is good, and you can make a short prayer in your heart, recalling the presence of Jesus with you wherever you are. Finally, using these meditations is a beginning, not an end. Once you have got used to the method, you can use the scriptures to develop your prayer life in your own way. There are also some notes after the meditations with suggestions for following the way of prayer further.

Pattern and Growth

While it is not essential to follow the order of the meditations, they are intended to develop sequentially. Those in Part 1 are about developing the relationship with Jesus anew, stepping into the light of his love, and bringing fresh light into your prayer life. Part 2 is mainly concerned with tuning your will to that of Jesus, learning to follow his will, his way, in obedience and discipleship. Part 3 is intended to lead to a deeper relationship with Jesus, to love him with all your heart. The meditations in this group tend to be more reflective with more space and silence, thus laying the foundations for developing your prayer life from thinking and imagining into stillness and being.

MEDITATIONS

PART ONE

DEVELOPING THE RELATIONSHIP WITH JESUS

Step into the light
Of a new reality
It doesn't matter what you are
Or what you used to be
He loved you from the start
His love can change your heart
Step into a new reality.

—Susie Hare, from "Step Into the Light"

1. LIFTED BY FRIENDS

LUKE 5:17-26

There's a person who has been paralyzed all her life. She can't do anything for herself, so life can be pretty bleak. She relies on others to feed her, wash her, dress her, and see to all her bodily needs. Fortunately, she has some good friends who look after her. They take her around with them, trying to include her in whatever they are doing. One day, they hear about a healer in their district, so they decide to pick up their friend on her bed and carry her to where the healer is, in someone's house. There's such a crowd they can't get anywhere near the door, let alone inside to meet the healer. They don't give up; rather than pack up and go home they decide to get their friend to this healer by making a hole in the roof and lowering her down inside. What happens then is more of a surprise than they'd bargained for. First the healer says something about the forgiveness of sins—which causes some serious muttering among the officials who happened to be around. Then, as if that is not enough, he tells the paralyzed person, "Stand up! And pick up your bedding, and walk!" And they are all stunned with amazement when she does stand up, and picks up the bedroll, and walks out of the door!

Meditation

You are the paralyzed person—be that person.

Feel what it is to be flat on your back, unable to move your limbs.

You can do nothing for yourself. Imagine your friends getting you up in the morning, washing your face, and hands, putting your clothes on.

Then feeding you your breakfast.

Life is not a lot of fun. Feel the restrictions—your friends can get about, have freedom, can work, can dance, can play. Not you.

Feel what it is like—to be carried everywhere, helpless; having to ask for a drink, to be turned over in bed, for more clothes or fewer.

You have four very good friends. You are fortunate. They must love you a lot to do so much for you, to limit their own freedom. Perhaps you can give them names.

Picture your friends around you: being patient; talking to you; listening to you; thinking of ways to help and support you.

Now comes a different sort of day. They tell you about a healer in town; they've heard he can cure sick people, and they want to take you to him.

You feel doubtful; who ever heard of a paralyzed person being cured? It's never happened.

You resist. Imagine yourself saying things like: "Please don't trouble. It's not worth it." What else might you be saying? What are you feeling?

They insist. And they're so good to you, that you feel you must go along with the idea, but you can't see anything coming of it.

So now you are being carried by your four friends, one at each corner of your bed-roll; you are carried down the main street. You are used to being carried around.

You arrive at the house where the healer is supposed to be.

What a crowd! You don't like crowds. Look at the place: it's crammed, the door is blocked, people are crowding the windows.

So that's all right, you think, no chance of getting near. You don't have to go through the embarrassment after all; you can just go home, do something else.

Oh no! They won't be put off by a crowd! They really are determined to get you in. You hear them discussing: "Get some ropes"—"Climb on the roof"—"One at each corner."

To your surprise and horror, two of your friends are climbing up to the roof. Now they are lifting off some of the big tiles, making a hole, passing the tiles down to the other two. What an embarrassment!

Now, help! Horrors! They are lifting you up to the roof. Feel yourself being hoisted up; they've got a rope at each corner of the bed-roll. What a terrifying experience!

Feel the terror as they lower you down—and down.

And down—to the floor.

Into the middle of this crowd, all these faces looking down at you; the surprise and disdain written on them.

Feel the shame and embarrassment, the fear, the anxiety.

All those faces.

One face is different.

You feel you know who this is.

He is calm. He breathes peace and stillness.

He radiates confidence, and joy.

Your fears evaporate; you breathe the calm.

He speaks: "Your sins are forgiven," he says.
Strange—you feel totally relaxed, cleansed, at one with him.
Let his peace and love flow over you.

There is some muttering in the background, which you hardly hear. And he stills it at once and turns to you.
"Stand up," he says, "pick up your bedding; and then go home!"
You feel a sort of shock. It's like a dream. But it's so real. You can do it!

You do exactly as he says.
He fills you with confidence . . . you can stand.
Feel yourself standing; for the first time. You feel strong, and upright.
You trust him absolutely. You roll up the bedding, and pick it up, glancing up at your good friends with heartfelt gratitude.
You are overwhelmed with joy . . . your heart is full. Stay in stillness with Jesus who is joy and peace and love.

Debriefing/Reflection

Now reflect on your thoughts and feelings. What is in your heart at this time?

What are you aware of? What was your reaction to this event?

Perhaps Jesus is healing something within you.

What is it in our lives that paralyzes us? Fear? Lack of self-love? Lack of confidence? Negative feelings of all kinds? Sense of failure?

Can we bring these things to Jesus? Does Jesus heal us? (Remember that the New Testament word for "heal" is the same as the word for "save.")

What experiences have we had of being released from bonds of fear in our lives?

Some have said that fear is the greatest block to spiritual growth. And "perfect love casts out fear" (1 John 4:18).

2. OUT OF HOPELESSNESS, INTO LIFE

LUKE 17:11-19

Leprosy is one of the worst things that could happen to anyone (it used to be incurable—a bit like AIDS). Anyone who caught this dreadful disease developed creeping skin sores which gradually ate away at their limbs. Worse still, they became outcasts because no one else wanted to catch it from them. So they had to leave home and family, keeping clear of other people—except other lepers—and live in groups or colonies. They couldn't work but relied on begging or scrounging for scraps to eat. A terrible, heartbreaking existence: no family, no friends, no purpose for living, no end in sight—except a slow death.

One colony of ten lepers had been around for some time, living this slow death. They were a mixed group, which meant that they weren't all orthodox Jews; some were Samaritans, doubly outcast because normally Jews would have nothing to do with them. They were near the high road, hoping for money and scraps from travelers. One day they heard that a so-called healer was coming by on his way from Galilee to Jerusalem.

So they stood at a distance from the roadside and called out to him: "Jesus, Master, have pity on us." He heard their calls, but he didn't say, "Be cured" or anything. He simply said, "Go and show yourselves to the priests" (the equivalent of saying, "Go and report to the local health authority representatives to get signed off"). So they went on their way, and as they walked they suddenly saw that the leprosy was gone—they were cleansed.

Now nine out of the ten continued on their way rejoicing. But one, who was a double outcast, Samaritan and leper, turned back. He came to Jesus praising God, and fell down on his knees at Jesus' feet, thanking him. And Jesus was a bit surprised, because he'd cured ten lepers, but only one, a double outcast at that, had bothered to come back and say thank you. And Jesus said an interesting thing to that person: "Stand up and go on your way; your faith has made you whole." Nine were "cured," but the tenth leper was made whole!

Meditation

You are the leper, the double outcast, Samaritan as well as leper.
  Try to imagine what this means.

Outcast means you are unwanted; cut off.
Cut off from family. Cut off from friends.
You are in a country of strangers, people who don't want you anyway.
Try to feel the loneliness, frightening loneliness, being outside every-thing that's going on.
You feel, "I'm not wanted. People hate me."

You've got to survive somehow, to find enough to eat.
Picture yourself begging from passers-by, pleading, groveling.
Or searching for scraps of food on the waste dumps.
You have some companions: there are ten of you (you may name some of them).
But you are rivals as well as friends in need; you all want the same scraps of food; you scramble for the same coins people throw.

And all the time you keep your distance; near enough the main road to shout to people, not too near to frighten them. No touching, no closeness.
And you have no hope, no future.
Feel the hopelessness of drifting downhill, the dreadful sores eating into you more and more. A living death; but only death will end it.

One day there's a ray of hope, which may or may not fade like the other faint rays.
A gaggle of people trickling along the main road to Jerusalem.
Not keeping a steady pace, like most travelers; they move haphazardly, and keep stopping.

And you can see someone in the middle, a central figure who stops and talks to people on the way. Discusses, points, touches.
What's it all about? you ask; someone has heard that this person is a great healer.
Some chance, you think, who ever heard of a leper being cleansed? Ah well, try anything.
What's he called? "Jesus," someone says.

You all agree to shout to him together—keeping your distance, of course.
So all together: "Jesus, Master, have pity on us!"
Heads turn; a bit disapproving perhaps. But you shout again, louder.
This time Jesus turns, and looks at you. Even at that distance, say forty or fifty paces, you have a sense of something, someone, different.
There's a moment's silence. You feel . . . power . . . joy . . .
Then he speaks, and surprises you all.
He simply says, "Go and show yourselves to the priests."

27

No one argues, no one says a word. You are all stunned.
Almost mechanically, you all turn and go, head for the town.
And as you go, surprise, joy, incredulity—your leprosy is cleansed!
Can this be true? Yes; your skin is new. In fact you feel new, a new person!

You pause, overcome with amazement, as it sinks in—slowly.
Then you have a very important impulse. This is someone very exceptional.
The others go on. You turn back to Jesus. You go to him.
And all the time you are shouting out—aloud or inside you—"Praise God! Thank you, God! Praise God for his goodness!"
And you kneel down at Jesus' feet, and say, "Thank you Lord, thank you Jesus," over and over.
And Jesus holds his hand out to you. He says, "I thought ten were cleansed; I wonder where the other nine are. Has only this double outcast come back to say thank you?"
And then he says to you, "Go on your way. In turning to me you have been made whole, healed inwardly as well as outwardly."

But you stay with him awhile.
What do you feel? Maybe tears of joy and gratitude fill your eyes.
It's so hard to realize the wonderful thing that has happened to you. He has released you out of hopelessness and into life. Made you a new person.
Rest in that for a time.

Debriefing/Reflection

How did you respond to this? What were your feelings?

Did you feel a sense of renewal?

Could you feel the joy and the thankfulness of the leper?

Have people in the group ever sensed the loneliness of the leper? A sense of being out of things, cut off? What have been the circumstances?

What about the inner healing, wholeness? What does this mean for us?

What about the feelings of thankfulness when Jesus is able to transform life?

3. TAKING CHAOS, MAKING PEACE

MATTHEW 9:23-27

The fishermen who had, for the time being, left their nets to be with Jesus had had a busy day. Exercising crowd control—and what crowds! People pushing to be near Jesus, trying to hear him, to receive his healing touch. As the sun was dipping, Jesus called it a day, and with Peter, James, Andrew, and John got into the boat and set off for the far side of the lake. All was now wonderfully peaceful, and Jesus, exhausted, lay down in the stern of the boat and went to sleep.

Then one of those really nasty, sudden storms got up from nowhere. One minute it was calm, the next the wind rose, creating frantic noise and vicious waves. The boat became hard to control, battered by the waves. All the experienced strength of the fishermen was tested in trying to keep the boat's head to wind and waves. But it was not enough and the boat began to fill with water.

In desperation they called to Jesus to help them. And he, even before he got to his feet, reproached them for lack of faith! Then he sternly rebuked the wind and the waves. And amazingly the storm calmed down as quickly as it had arisen.

As the wind and the waves died away, they felt a deep sense of calm, and an even deeper sense of awe. Who could this be that even the winds and the waves obeyed him?

Meditation

Picture a scene by a lakeside. Swirling crowds, constantly moving, everyone trying to get to the center. Pushing, jostling, always on the move.

And at the epicenter Jesus: calm, loving, open, and touching each in need with healing power, and a tender word.

Not all are good-tempered; mixed motives are at play. Some are just curious, looking for the new—sensation seekers and attention seekers.

Others are desperate for help, and many have come to hear him talk, to drink at this well of refreshing waters.

Now choose to be one of four disciples: Peter, James, Andrew, or John.

It's been a hot and busy day. Crowds pressing all the time, people call-ing for attention. Desperately trying to be fair to all, to bring the most needy to Jesus. To cope with the pushy people who don't really need any-thing at all, and the constant clamor for attention. Noisy, sweaty, hectic.

Here's a woman with her crippled son; a blind man in rags; a person covered in sores. And so they keep coming and asking, pleading, demand-ing.

Imagine how you feel as the day comes to an end, really knocked out. Oh, for some peace!

Now picture the four of you getting into the boat with Jesus. If you're exhausted, he is totally washed out, has given everything to people throughout the long day.

And you feel pleased that he settles down to sleep in the stern with his head on a cushion.

The boat is your natural environment; you are at home on the water. You relax immediately as you push off from the shore, and settle into the gentle swing of the oars; the rhythm has a wonderfully calming effect. Peace, tranquillity, bliss—feel the freshness, the calm, the lulling gentle rhythm of the oars.

The evening sky is clear; there's not a breath of wind—well, hardly a breath.

Actually the wind is beginning to stir a little as it does at this time of day. Refreshing, a welcome cooling.

In fact it's moving quite a lot, whipping up little wavelets. Still, that's noth-ing unusual. There's often an evening breeze.

Well, it is a bit unusual; the wind is building more strongly now; maybe one of those freak storms is brewing—but they blow out quickly, so you just press on.

But the wind seems to be getting up more than usual, driving bigger waves towards the boat. You'll have to pull against the wind and waves.

Now it really is beginning to be a storm. Black clouds are racing across the sky. The wind is rising more and more. The waves are growing too; nasty steep waves slapping against the sides of the boat.

Not so much slapping as crashing against the sides of the boat.

You'll have to get the boat's head to the wind, just to be on the safe side. This is beginning to be tricky. Feel the first prickle of fear.

Now the wind is raging ferociously, the noise is frantic. The waves are building up ever more, taller than the boat. The waves are spilling water into the boat.

This is no ordinary storm; feel the fear rising in you.

The noise is now terrifying; the wind is screaming, huge waves are crashing into the boat. Water is slopping about in the boat, making it lower in the water and even more vulnerable.

Panic sets in. You'll sink if this goes on.

You and the others shout to each other but can't hear.

What can you do? You're desperate.

You will have to wake Jesus and get his help.

"Jesus!" you shout. "Jesus! Help us, Master, we're sinking. Help!"

In spite of the deafening noise, you hear him say quite gently: "Where is your faith?"

Then, to your horror and amazement, he stands up!

"Be still," he says to the winds and waves. "Be quite still."

Immediately the wind begins to ease—from a screaming demon, it gently dies down.

As it drops to a sigh, the waves begin to settle down, and take on some sort of order before they fall quite flat. And the clouds scud away, one by one, over the horizon.

As the last clouds disappear, the late evening sun kisses the water again.

And there is a great calm; a heavenly stillness.

Sense the utter peace and tranquillity.

Who is this who takes chaos and makes peace?

Debriefing/Reflection

Our lives are often chaos, a jumble. Sometimes that is our doing, sometimes it comes from factors outside us; and sometimes both. The result is stress.

Were you able to let Jesus create calm in that meditation?

How can you find ways of letting Jesus come into your chaos and give you peace?

[Note: this is a good meditation to use when you are kept awake by overwhelming worries and anxieties. Jesus takes chaos and makes peace.]

4. A NEW HEART

LUKE 19:1-10

There was once a man who was part of the corrupt tax system—hated because he worked for the enemy occupying power *and* because he twisted the rules to make a good bit extra for himself. He didn't mind being unpopular because he made so much money. Or perhaps he was so intent on making money it hadn't dawned on him just how badly he was treating people.

One day there was a bit of a circus in town. Or so it seemed to Zacchaeus (that was his name), and he thought he'd better have a look and see what all the fuss was about. Some traveling preacher (huh!) who seemed to have influenced a great many people—maybe he could teach Zacchaeus a trick or two. As he was very short (say four foot eleven) he couldn't see a thing over the heads of the crowd. So he climbed a tree, a rather handy tree, and got a good view.

Then he got the shock of his life. As Jesus came level with him, he looked straight into his eyes and said to him, "Come on down—I'm going to have supper with you and stay at your house." Something happened to Zacchaeus from that moment; he came down, raced back to his house, organized a really good meal, and welcomed Jesus (there was some disapproval from the "proper" sorts of people, who understandably didn't think much of Zacchaeus). But as they sat down, Zacchaeus, deeply moved by his meeting with Jesus, stood up, and promised to change everything—to give away half his wealth and repay four times over everyone he'd cheated. And Jesus said, "Today salvation (meaning wholeness, new life) has come to this house."

Meditation

You could try to be Zacchaeus but his job was locked into his time, making it hard for us to know what it was really like. So if you find it too hard to imagine, then be yourself.

Now, try to think of what it is in your life that might block you from seeing the truth about yourself as Jesus sees you.

Maybe you don't know of anything; if so, just imagine a block and let Jesus show you if there really is anything. It could, for example, be fear, anxiety, low self-esteem, unwillingness to accept forgiveness or to forgive others.

When you are ready, try to be part of that scene. Perhaps choose a place, a road, you know.
Picture the crowds along the road, heaving with people; a real crush.
Many are standing at the roadside just looking on. Others are trying to push through to get to the front.
There's a solid mass of people.
They are blocking your view. You can't see through them, or around them.

Panic. What can you do? You are truly desperate to catch a glimpse of this man.
And you are far too short to see over them.
You really, really want to see and the tall people in front are stopping you.
So you must find a way to get higher, must climb somehow.

You look round for a wall, a fence. Nothing.
A tree—yes, find a tree. None at hand. You are going to miss him if you don't hurry. You go down the road.
There's one, plenty of good low branches.
Up you go. That's more like it.

Now you are up in the tree and have a really good view.
Yes, you can see a group of people meandering along the road.
And in the middle is Jesus . . .
What is he doing? Talking with the people around. Imagine him as he moves along.

He comes level with you. He seems to be looking at you. He is looking at you.
Now—a real surprise—he's looking straight into your eyes, deep into you.
"Help!" you think. "What does he see?"
Let him show you. Maybe take some time to work out your own feelings as he looks into your heart, and sees—what?
His gaze is searching. He sees deep into you, but he also loves you.
Feel his love enfolding you.

When you feel ready, hear him call your name: "I want to come and be with you; I want to live in your life . . ."
Choose how you respond to him.

Imagine him coming into your house, to be with you.
Imagine him sitting down with you.

As he sits with you, and looks into your heart, you may become aware of something—small or large—which may block your closeness to him; which holds you back.

Perhaps he shows you something which had eluded you: a sin, bitterness, a reluctance to forgive, a limitation on your commitment to him.
Let him touch and heal whatever it is.

You may want to say something to him . . . to welcome him, to ask him to be part of your life, or to change some aspect of your life.

He brings you great love—the healing and wholeness that is his gift for making us new people.
Perhaps take some time to reflect, to thank him, to bask in his love.

Debriefing/Reflection

How do you respond to this meeting with Jesus?
What is Jesus saying to you?
What changes does he want to make in your life?
What are your feelings? Do you feel closer to Jesus?

5. OUT OF DARKNESS, INTO HIS MARVELOUS LIGHT

MARK 10:46-52

Note: This meditation becomes more effective if those taking part have had an experience of "blindness" beforehand, for example, trying to eat something with a knife and fork while blindfolded, with someone else giving instructions.

A young man, blind from an early age, was learning just how tough life could be. His name was Bartimaeus, and he lived with his parents in the large town of Jericho. They were very poor, and though they had brought him up, they could no longer afford to feed him. So there was only one thing for it—he had to beg for his living. That meant sitting at the roadside, calling out to passers-by for money or food. A harsh life, with little to look forward to—maybe starvation when his parents died, then sickness and death. A bleak future.

One day, as he sat and begged, he became aware of a large crowd heading out of town, and asked people around what it was about.

"Oh, someone called Jesus of Nazareth," they said, "supposed to be a prophet and healer." Prophet and healer, he thought; this is my big opportunity. So he yelled out from where he sat at the back of the crowd, "Jesus, Son of David, have pity on me."

The people around turned on him and told him to be quiet. But he was so convinced that Jesus could help him that he shouted even more loudly, "Jesus, Jesus, Son of David, have pity on me."

And Jesus heard him. And told his followers, "Call him here." So Bartimaeus stood up, his cloak falling to the ground, and hands pushed him through the crowd to Jesus.

"Well," said Jesus, "what do you want me to do for you?" (Knowing full well, as he always does.)

"Master, let me see again," pleaded Bartimaeus.

"Go on your way," said Jesus. "Your faith has made you whole!"

And *at once* his sight came back. And didn't he just dance for joy!

Meditation

You are blind, living in a world of which you can see nothing, which is also a world of sounds. You must be sensitive to sounds, and to spaces.

Hear the faint sounds which are always there. Feel the spaces around you.

All your life you have been led from place to place, helped with food, with dressing, with finding water to drink. In this harsh world where the disadvantaged are condemned rather than supported, life has been a string of clumsiness, of spillage, of bumping into people and things.

And waiting impatiently for people to help.

Now as a young adult you try to be as independent as possible, resisting too much help, frustrated with the difficulty of getting things right.

Feel the resentment, the frustrations, sometimes bitterness.

Your parents are poor, and help you as they can. In a harsh world there's only one way to survive as an adult who cannot work. No one will give you a job; there's nothing useful you can do. So you feel useless, discarded, unwanted.

So you must beg; suffer the indignity. At least you can't see people's faces—though sometimes your keen ears pick up the sneering remarks.

Picture yourself: each day you find your way out of the gate and to a place near the side of the main road. Each day you listen for footsteps and call out for money and food.

"Please help a poor blind man." Sometimes there's a curse, and sometimes a coin chinks into your bowl; sometimes a piece of bread.

And always you say, "Thank you, and blessings on you." But it's a dreary life stretching out before you, little hope, little future.

One day is different from the rest. A cool day, you hug your thin cloak around you. But there seems to be more of a crowd coming by; your ears pick up the sound of many feet. Something is happening, your ears catch a stir of activity outside the gate. What is it?

You ask the people around you, "What's going on?"

"It's some guy from Nazareth," they say. "A traveling preacher. Quite a prophet and healer, so some say."

A prophet and healer. Surely he can help you. A tinge of excitement mixed with fear touches you. This may be your only chance for a change in your life.

How can you get his attention? He's in the middle of that crowd, somewhere.

You must get his attention, let him know your plight. You will have to be bold and shout out to him; you'll have to call very loudly. You yell, "Jesus, Son of David, have pity on me."

People turn round and hiss at you. "For goodness' sake be quiet," they say. "Who do you think you are? Don't waste his time, he's got better things to do."

What can you do? you wonder. Imagine your feelings.

He hasn't heard you; the opportunity is slipping away as the crowd moves on along the road.
You'll have to shout again, more loudly—never mind the people around.
"Jesus, Lord Jesus, Son of David, have pity on me."

No hissing at you this time. The movement of the crowd stops.
There's a pause, a hush. Will anything happen?
You pick up a quietly spoken order, "Bring him to me."
"You're in luck," someone says. As you stand and let your cloak slip off, you feel hands pushing you forward, leading you through the crowd.
You sense a quietness, an expectation in the crowd.
You also sense a very different kind of presence. You feel excitement, awe, a little fear. And hope.

When Jesus speaks, his voice carries warmth, joy, hope. "What is it that you want from me?" he says.
You gulp, feelings overwhelming you.
You find your voice. "Lord," you say, "please may I have my sight back?" A pause. Silence. Will anything happen? you wonder.

Then those astonishing words, "You shall have your sight back. Your faith has healed you."
And suddenly you are dazzled by light, glorious light; the incredible sight of people and trees. And at the center, most dazzling of all, is Jesus. You are overcome with joy and delight.
All around, people are praising God and sharing in your joy.
Most wonderful of all is the way you feel totally renewed by Jesus—an extraordinary transformation. You feel you have stepped out of darkness into his marvelous light.

Debriefing/Reflection

Have you experienced a time when your eyes were opened to some new light from Jesus Christ? Or a new insight?

Many Christians have an experience of being in a kind of spiritual darkness. What has been your experience? And have you come through a time of darkness with greater light at the end?

Jesus says, "I am the light of the world" (John 8:5). How does this help your understanding of Jesus?

6. Making Gifts Work

JOHN 6:1-14

One day, when Jesus was teaching in a rather out-of-the-way place, people came traipsing out to see and hear him in large numbers. Curiosity, attraction, searching for something new—who knows? But there they were.

After he had been teaching for some time, Jesus saw that the people were clearly tired, and needed food in order to go on.

So Jesus said to his disciples, "It's time to eat; would you please find some food for these people?" And of course the disciples told him there was no way they could buy enough food for so many people, even if they were in reach of the stores.

One of them, Andrew, spotted a youngster with a picnic and reported, "There is someone here with food, but nothing like enough." Jesus just told them to sit everyone down. And he took the one-person picnic, a couple of little bread rolls and some fish, and said the blessing. Then the disciples took the food, and shared it all around. To their great surprise, everyone had a good meal, and there was some left over!

Meditation

You are in your childhood, quite young, say twelve or so. Living in the country, you can enjoy going off for the day exploring the surrounding countryside which is, of course, quite safe.

So, one day you set off with a modest picnic and a little water from the well. You follow the stream uphill. Picture the scene as you meander up the edge of the stream. You delight in the bright sunshine, sparkling water, trees dressed in green, birds singing.

Feel the gentle and joyful happiness, and the utter peace; and the sense that you have all this space.

Higher up, you move away from the stream, and round the side of the hill. An astonishing sight greets your eyes!

People, hundreds of people—and in this out-of-the-way place! What are they doing here? you wonder. Surely no one ever comes here from the towns; you've never seen anyone out here before.

Then you see him. Further up the hill; he's standing there, the focus of attention. In fact the crowds are all quite silent and still, listening to him. Extraordinary, so many people being quiet and attentive.

You ask someone about him, and learn that his name is Jesus. He is much admired as a prophet and teacher.

You move to get nearer, threading your way through the crowds, until you are quite close. And you listen, enthralled. No one ever spoke like this before.

You are astonished at what he says.

"The poor are much blessed. The Kingdom of Heaven is for them," he says.

The poor? Blessed? What can he mean by that? Surely they're poor because they're bad and lazy?

Yet he speaks with great authority, and the huge crowd is very still and seems to respect him.

"Love your enemies," he is saying. What? Surely you attack your enemies—the hated occupying soldiers, for a start. Why not take revenge?

"Do good to those that hate you." What can he mean? We usually hate back, with interest. An eye for an eye, a tooth for a tooth, that's our way of doing things.

There's a pause. He's saying something to one of his friends. You are quite close to them now, and hear something about "time to get everyone some food." His friend seems to demur—no money, and anyway the shops are out of reach. We can't possibly feed so many people. One or two might have some food, not that it would be enough.

Your ears prick up. I've got a picnic, but only for me. That won't go far. What am I meant to do? Give it away and starve? Maybe split it into two.

The friend spots you. "Let's see what you've got," he asks—very kindly and gently.

Not much; a couple of crusty rolls—little home-baked loaves—and a few small fish.

They confer again, and now his friends are getting everyone to sit down.

You hand over your precious picnic.

Jesus says the blessing, "Blessed are you, O Lord our God, King Eternal, who brings bread from the earth," and he breaks the little bread loaves and starts to put the pieces into the baskets his friends have. He does the same with the fish.

Now comes the part you will never forget. They start to hand out bread and fish to some of the people as they sit, men and women and some children. They can't go far with that small amount.

In fact that must surely be as far as it will go.

You think, what about my turn? If they go on giving it out I won't get any of my own picnic.

How do you feel about losing your meal?

But then they go on passing food out to people; surely it should have been used up long ago.

And still they hand out food; and more and more, on and on. They all seem to have some, it never runs out. Now your turn comes, and you get your share; more even than you brought with you!

Your little picnic for one has become food for many.

Who is this? Who can he be? you ask yourself. How has he done this? Imagine your feelings.

No ordinary man. He's just sitting there quietly on a rock in the shade of a tree. As you look, wondering, he beckons you to come and sit by him. You wonder what this means.

A bit shy and a bit wary, you go and sit down. He looks at you very kindly. You warm to his look. It's friendly, loving, heart-warming.

He puts a hand on your shoulder and says, "You thought you had only a little gift to offer, didn't you? Hardly enough to be of any use. But God takes each gift you offer, and blesses it; and then it becomes enough, a gift for many people. One small gift is magnified hundreds of times by God's blessing. Now, go in peace, and be much blessed in your giving."

You are thrilled that God has taken your little picnic and used it to feed so many.

And you rest in his peace and his blessing, which will be with you always.

Debriefing/Reflection

Do you hold back from giving because you feel you have too little to give?

Perhaps you feel your own gifts and talents are too little, too small to be of any use?

How will the episode of the child's picnic being used for so many change the way you offer your gifts? And your talents?

Think about what your gifts and talents are, and try to recognize them. Try to identify each other's talents. Together you can offer them all to God.

7. ALL IS POSSIBLE

LUKE 7:1-10

One day when Jesus was traveling around Galilee, a Roman centurion whose servant was sick sent a message to Jesus asking him to come and heal the servant. The Jewish elders were in favor of Jesus going, because, unlike other Romans, this centurion had respect for the Jews and had even built a synagogue for them. So Jesus set out for the centurion's house. But as he got near, the centurion sent another message to him, saying, "Please don't trouble to come any further—I'm not worthy to have you in my house. I know that if you only say the word, my servant will be healed. I recognize your authority, because I know what authority means—I've got soldiers and servants under me who do whatever I tell them." And Jesus was amazed that a Roman should have such faith. "I tell you," he said, "I have not found such faith in Israel." And he spoke the word, and the servant was healed at that moment.

Meditation

You are one of the young servants, or rather a slave, in the household of a Roman centurion who is an important and wealthy man with much power. Many such Roman masters are cruel and harsh, often letting their chief steward beat the slaves for little or no reason.

Your master's name is Aquila, and unlike most other Roman masters he can be kind and even thoughtful. You are reasonably well fed and housed.

One of your fellow slaves is a great friend to you. You can give him or her a name, but we will simply refer to him or her as your friend. Picture the large stone-built house with its marble floors and, outside, the fine gardens.

You and the other slaves are up early, cleaning, cooking, washing, watering the garden, running errands. You and your friend are clearly trusted by your master.

So you work hard, but you can also picture yourself in the scorching heat of the afternoon sitting with your friend on the edge of the garden— the master is on duty with the soldiers at the garrison, and the mistress is having her afternoon sleep. Not a bad life for a slave, especially when compared with many other Roman households. You have a sense of contentment, and are grateful to have such a good friend.

One afternoon, your friend is very unwell with a painful head, feeling burning hot. You help him or her to lie down on the mat in the outbuilding where you sleep. You get something to drink, and try to bathe that painful head.

Worrying. You feel helpless. Perhaps one of the maids will tell the mistress when she wakes up.

As the afternoon wears on, your friend, now only half-conscious and becoming delirious, gets worse, the fever hotter than ever. You are now quite fearful.

The mistress has no interest—slaves fall ill and die; it's just one of those things. You are sick with anxiety, and impatient for the master to get home, because you know he cares for his slaves.

Imagine your feelings, your fear, your anxiety.

At long last he is home, and fortunately someone has the sense to tell him straight away of your friend's sickness. He takes one look at this sick slave, and then issues you with orders.

Roman masters don't bother with a doctor for slaves, but you are somewhat surprised at the orders he gives you.

"There is a great and good Jewish healer in the town," he says. "You are to go to him. His name is Jesus, and you will probably find him in the market square—but you will know where he is by the crowds around him. When you find him, be very respectful, make your bow, and ask him if he would please come to the house and heal my slave."

You run as fast as you can, glad to be doing something but filled with fear. Will you find Jesus? Will you be able to get near him to speak? Will he listen, and most important will he actually come to a Roman household?

Breathless, you reach the market square. It is packed with people; but in the far corner you catch a glimpse of someone who seems to be speaking to the crowds. That must surely be him, but how can you possibly get near?

You start to worm your way through the crush; sometimes you must ask people to let you, a slave, pass through. "Please, I have an urgent message from my master to give to Jesus." Hot and breathless, you find yourself at the front of the crowd, facing Jesus. No mistaking him; he is quite unlike any person you have ever seen. He breathes grace and authority.

People look at you—haughtily—a slave, dirty and sweaty. Yet you must fulfill your errand.

You bow low, as you have been taught. "Please, Lord Jesus, my master Aquila begs that you will come to his house and heal his servant who is very sick." You say the words with desperation.

Will he listen? Will he come to the house?

To your surprise, voices speak up; not, as you might have expected, to deride talk of going to a Roman household, but in support. They are Jewish elders. "He is a good and worthy man," they are saying. "He even built our synagogue."

"Please come," you find yourself saying. "It's my friend who is sick."

"Yes," says Jesus, "of course I will come."

What joy! There may be hope for your friend.

The elders even agree to accompany Jesus; they seem very confident in his powers to heal.

You run on ahead to tell your master. Some of the anxiety is diminished. But you wonder, can Jesus really make your friend well again?

You arrive back at the house, even more breathless, and report to your master that Jesus has agreed to come.

Your master surprises you again.

"He is a good and holy man; he must not have the fact that he entered a Roman household held against him. You are to go to him and greet him at the gateway, and this is the message you are to give him from me:

Lord Jesus, please trouble to come no further, for I am not worthy to have you under my roof—which is why I did not presume to come to you in person. You need only speak the word and my slave will be healed. I can recognize authority when I see it, for I too have authority, with soldiers and slaves under me; I have only to speak and they will obey.' "

"Now make sure you get that exactly right; and be very respectful as before."

Extraordinary—all this from a Roman centurion of all people.

You run to the gateway, and see Jesus and the elders approaching. You bow low again as instructed, and then you give Jesus the message exactly as your master told you.

And you wait, anxiously; what will Jesus say to this?

But he smiles at you—encouragement—and then turns to the people following him and says: "Do you hear this, all of you? Nowhere have I met faith like this, not in the length and breadth of Israel!"

Turning back to you, he says: "Your friend is well; you may go now. May peace and blessings go with you."

You bow low again, and with joy, hardly believing what you have heard, you run back to the house.

And there in the garden you see your friend, fit and well and smiling, the master's hand on one shoulder. He too is beaming; perhaps there's a tear trickling down his face.

What wonders you have seen and heard; this you will never forget.

How can you learn more of Jesus, who heals with a word?

But meanwhile you bask in the joy of your friend's recovery, and in the peace and blessing of Jesus.

Debriefing/Reflection

How do you understand faith?

To many it is simply the same as trust, and can be bigger or smaller.

In the New Testament, the word for "faith" and the word for "believe" are the same; in essence they describe a relationship to God in trust and obedience, through the saving acts of Jesus.

What does this mean for us in our prayers of intercession? Prayers for the sick, for example?

What can we learn from the centurion and his slave?

8. Reversal

O ne day as Jesus taught in the temple courtyard, the Pharisees thought they had really caught him out. They brought a woman and stood her in front of Jesus. "This woman," they said, "has been caught in the very act of committing adultery." And they challenged Jesus, "In the Law of Moses we are commanded that she must be stoned to death. Now what do you say?"

Jesus ignored them, but wrote with his finger on the ground (much to their annoyance). So they went on questioning him for his opinion on what should be done.

Eventually he straightened up, and returned their challenge: "Let anyone among you who is without sin cast the first stone." And then he went on writing with his finger on the ground. Of course they all slunk off, beginning with the oldest, and left the woman standing there on her own.

Jesus asked the woman, "Where are they? Has no one condemned you?"

She said, "No one, Sir."

And Jesus said, "Well neither do I condemn you; go your way and don't sin again."

Meditation

It's one of those warm, sunny days, fresh without being too hot. You are sitting near Jesus in the temple courtyard, listening to him teaching. He always teaches by telling stories, sometimes giving the old stories a completely new twist. Really eye-opening.

Imagine yourself sitting there among a group of his followers, drinking in those refreshing parables, entranced by wonderful new insights.

"Once upon a time there was a very rich man, who got richer and richer. And he thought to himself, 'What I need to do is to build even bigger barns, then I can store up all I need, and live a life of luxury forever.' And he was rubbing his hands in glee, when God said to him, 'You fool, this very night your life will be taken, and what use will all your riches and stores be to you then?'"

At that moment, there is an interruption: the Pharisees again—they're the guardians of the religious Law which governs every detail of life—pedantic men concerned with the letter of the Law.

They've really got it in for Jesus. Feel the resentment combined with anxiety rising in you. One day, you fear they will surely find him out.

This time, they've got two of the temple guards with them—big brutes. They drag a poor woman into the middle of the people sitting around Jesus, and leave her standing there, disheveled, distraught and covered in confusion and shame.

The temple guards look smug.

"Now then," says one of the Pharisees, "answer this if you can. This woman was caught in the very act of adultery. You know the Law of Moses; it says she must be stoned to death. No exceptions allowed. So what do you say to that, Teacher?" The speaker adds a note of sarcasm.

"Will you join us in fulfilling the Law?"

They've really caught him now. He can't deny the Law, it's absolutely sacred. If he tries to stop them, they'll put him up against the wall with her and stone him as well.

Whatever will he do now?

Imagine your fear for him. There's no way out of this.

To your amazement, Jesus ignores them. He just leans over as he sits, and writes in the dust with his finger. Aramaic, difficult to read upside down. Something about the plank in your eye and the speck of sawdust in the other's.

What are you feeling? She has flouted the Law with scandal. Does she deserve punishment?

The Pharisees bang on about the Law. "No answer then, Master. Better move over and we can put her up against that wall."

The temple guards look eager; one of them even has a stone ready in his hand.

This has got to be it. Feel the fear grip you as you realize that Jesus has no answer.

Jesus hardly looks up as, at last, he speaks. But the words, quietly spoken, seem to ring like a series of bell-notes: "Let the one of you who has no sin cast the first stone."

And he bends to write again. Something like "Don't judge, or you will be judged."

Silence. Absolute silence . . . tense . . . prickly.

The guards look crestfallen. The Pharisees look stunned.
The oldest of them pulls his cloak around him, and walks off—rather stiffly.
Another silence. Then another Pharisee leaves. And after a pause, a third.
Finally the one who challenged Jesus beckons to the guards with his head and they, too, leave.

At last Jesus sits up very straight. He looks at the woman.
Now this is something you will never forget. As he looks at her, he seems to enfold her in the most amazing, forgiving love; a kind of warm, life-enhancing, supportive love.

Difficult to describe, but the effect is miraculous. As she stands there, she loses her haunted, hunted look. You see her seem to straighten up, grow taller, no longer clutching her thin clothes around her. Even her face, which had been narrow and sunken, seems to fill out. The shame falls away.
She looks gratefully, almost confidently, at Jesus.
"No one has condemned you then?" he asks.
"No sir," she says, "no one."
"Well," says Jesus, "I certainly don't condemn you. Now go in peace, and let sin rule over you no more."
She goes down on one knee, and kisses Jesus' feet. Then she goes quietly on her way with a wonderful look of serene joy on her face.

You pause to think. That tells you everything about Jesus. He forgives. He restores. He makes new.
What do you think and feel now?
Do you think, "I am a sinful person. Surely I, too, should stand there in front of Jesus, where that woman was"?

If that is what you think and feel, then get up and stand there on exactly the same spot as the woman.
Let Jesus see right through you. He looks at you as he looked at that woman.
Feel that warm, forgiving love embrace you, that supporting, life-enhancing love.
Feel that love enable you to stand tall and straight, confident in his grace empowering you—making you new.
And rest in that love.

Debriefing/Reflection

Do you find herself condemning other people for what you perceive as their sin?

Remember the saying of Jesus about "removing the plank from your eye before you tackle the speck of dust in the other person's eye" (Matthew 7:4).

How did Jesus' treatment of the woman affect you? And how will it change the way you think of other people?

How do you feel about standing in front of Jesus, like the woman?

To what extent are you able to accept the total and free forgiveness of God?

9. Life's Burden Lifted

LUKE 8:42*b*-48

Jammed in by the milling crowds, Jesus was trying to get to a house where someone's twelve-year-old daughter was dying. In the crowd was a woman who had suffered a dreadful bleeding for twelve years and spent all her money and more on doctors but without success. Presumably it was a hemorrhage from the womb, and under Jewish practice she would have been outcast, untouchable, all this time, and so have a sense of shame. The end of her money was the end of hope. Maybe Jesus could cure her. So she got through the crowds to him, and, not daring to speak for shame, or to touch his person, she just managed to touch the fringe of his cloak. And her bleeding stopped at that very moment.

But Jesus was aware and asked, "Who touched me?" Of course everyone around said, "Not me," but Peter, the practical one, said, "The crowds are crushed in here. There must be dozens of people who touched you."

Jesus was asking a different question. He knew that his power to heal had been tapped, and said so. At that the poor woman, terrified, trembling and covered in confusion, fell at his feet and explained, "It was me. All these years I have suffered shame and pain, and when I touched your cloak I was immediately healed."

And Jesus, who could see into the hearts of all, gave her his blessing. "Daughter," he said, "go in peace; your faith has made you whole."

And there Jesus used a wonderful word—in Greek *sozo*—which means both "healed" and "saved."

Meditation

You are in your early thirties, single, and employed—but only just. Since you were in your late teens you have carried a burden that has cost you friends and work. Round about the age of seventeen, a particularly tender, vulnerable age, a sore spot on your face—usually the sort that clears up— began to spread.

At first it was joked about, not always cruelly; but as it spread further over the side of your face, your friends began to stop asking you to meet them and made excuses when you asked them. Members of the opposite sex would have nothing to do with you.

Imagine some of the pain that you felt over this, the hurt, the isolation, and fear of the future.

And, illogically, of course, the shame; that worm of shame which can eat away at the heart and soul of people with visible disfigurements.

Since then, things have got steadily worse. At first you could cover the sore with a dressing, and at least you were able to get some work in an office. But gradually the sore spread to the whole of one side of your face.

Your GP tried various remedies, and then sent you to specialists. The answer was unhelpful: "It's caused by a virus, it will clear up in time. Let the sun and air get to it," they said, as if it were not already too widespread to cover with a dressing. "You'll just have to be patient."

In desperation you have tried all kinds of alternative medicines. Each has cost you money. You have spent all of your savings—all to no avail.

Life is almost unbearably painful. You have no friends. People shy away from you, frightened of catching something, frightened of disfigurement.

Imagine yourself in the streets, on the bus, being avoided; heads turn sometimes out of curiosity, sometimes disgust, rarely with compassion.

You are aware of people commenting to one another; you guess or over-hear the sometimes cruel things they say.

You can hear children whisper, half fascinated, half frightened.

Imagine your feelings. They may range between anger, helplessness, self-loathing, despair, depression and, above all, that terrible, corrosive shame.

Now, as a last resort, you decide to borrow money and spend it all on a specialist at the Mayo Clinic. He is the world expert on such problems.

A difficult decision, for his fee is substantial and you will be very poor for a very long time; but anything must be better than this burden. You have already moved from an apartment to a rented room and you are over-drawn at the bank.

You are walking through the streets and squares to make your way to the specialist, your scarf pulled up over your face to hide that terrible disfig-uring sore from people who shy away.

As you come into one of those elegant squares, you are surprised to find a large crowd moving slowly around it—not noisily—in fact, they seem quietly absorbed in moving toward the far corner.

The trees in the middle are a bright spring green in the warm sun; the buildings are tall and elegant.

You pause. You must get through to keep this expensive appointment, or all will be lost. But crowds are to be avoided; people cause you pain and are frightened of you.

They don't look violent, it's not a mob. Yet they seem to be moving with some sort of purpose. Maybe you can ask someone what it's all about.

There's a pleasant-looking lady nearby, and, keeping the bad side of your face away from her (as you have practiced for so long), you ask, "Excuse me, can you tell me what's going on here, please?"

She looks at you curiously, but not unkindly. "Why of course," she says, "I thought everybody knew about him. They're all following him. It's Jesus, the great prophet and healer. They say he's on his way to someone's little girl, who's dying."

Curious, you think. Well, yes, I know about Jesus, but I didn't know he was around here.

"Does he really heal people?" you ask.

"Oh yes!" she says. "He has wonderful powers. They say he comes from God himself."

More curious and more curious. You think, I wonder, could he cure even me?

Feel a mixture of doubt and hope building up in you.

There's nothing to lose, you think; and maybe, just maybe, a lot to gain. In any case, you still have to get through the crowd to keep your appointment.

You look at your watch; goodness, how time is rushing by, you must get on.

You start to work your way through the crowd toward the center.

It gets more and more dense, but you spot someone who is surely Jesus. He has an air of authority combined with compassion. Can he really help me? you wonder.

I need to get near him, you think. He looks kind. Actually he looks much more than kind. He looks so different that no words can describe him.

He is somehow otherworldly; there is a sense of power and radiance about him which draws out feelings of courage and faith. you feel sure that here is someone you can really trust. Blow the appointment, I really want to reach him.

At last you are close enough. Your intense shame and your fear of people overcome you.

You can't face him; the sense of shame and fear is too great.

You certainly can't touch him—people are terrified of your touch.

Perhaps you can try to touch the edge of his coat.

You creep up behind him, and reach out, fearful, your hand trembling.

You touch the very edge of his coat, all fear and trepidation.

For what seems a long moment, the world seems to be silent, to stand still.

Suddenly two things startle you in a mixture of joy and terror.

You instinctively put your hand to your face.

To your amazement you find that your face is completely clear—you touch new, clean skin such as you have not felt for many, many years.

At the same instant, Jesus turns around.

"Who touched me?" he says.

You are terrified. You try to sink back into the crowd; confusion and fear overwhelm you.

People are saying, "I didn't touch you," and, "Nor did I."

His friend says, "Come on, you must be joking. The crowd are nearly crushing you—they're all touching you."

But Jesus knows, and you know, that it was a different question he asked.

"Someone did touch me," he says. "I know that healing power has gone from me."

And he is looking straight at you. He can see right inside you; he knows you and understands all your problems.

He can see the years of cruel pain, the cancerous shame eating away at you, and the intense loneliness.

You feel found out, yet it is not an accusing look; rather understanding, even compassionate.

You fall at his feet, feeling a mixture of guilt and hope, fear and confusion.

And now you speak to him, "Lord Jesus, it was me. All these years I have suffered pain and shame. My life has not been worth living. And now I have been wonderfully healed. Please understand."

Jesus looks at you with marvelous tenderness and insight.

His look conveys infinite love, and he speaks words which will always live with you.

"Be at peace, child," he says. "You have faith, and faith has saved you, has made you whole. My blessing goes with you."

You stay close to him, dazed by the wonder and joy of his extraordinary love.

Debriefing/Reflection

Many people carry scars in their lives—not necessarily visible to others—often from childhood or the distant past. Maybe you have a burden of some kind, causing you pain, anxiety, problems with relationships, even unjustified feelings of guilt or shame.

Do you feel able to bring it to Jesus? To touch the hem of his cloak?

Can you identify with the woman who came to Jesus, trusting him as she did? Looking for that wholeness which only he can give?

10. A Surprise Visit

LUKE 24:33-43

After Jesus had been killed by his enemies, his followers went into hiding, fearing for their lives. There were strange rumors around. Peter claimed to have seen Jesus; so did Mary Magdalene, who had visited the tomb early in the morning and found it empty. Then two of his followers came back from a walk out of Jerusalem to their home. They said he had walked with them and spoken wonderfully about himself and the prophecies concerning his suffering and Resurrection. However, they had not recognized him until he had said the blessing over the bread at their meal.

While the disciples were in the midst of this discussion, Jesus came and stood in the middle of them and said, "Peace be with you." They were terrified, thinking he was a ghost. Jesus spoke to them, trying to reassure them: "Don't be frightened. Look at my hands and feet. You can see it is me. Touch me, and you will see that I am real." And he showed them his hands and his feet, with the marks of the nails.

They didn't know what to believe, hovering between joy and doubt. So while they were still wondering, he said, "Have you got anything to eat?" They gave him some fish, and he ate it in front of them. Then they had to believe he had risen from the dead!

Meditation

You are living in a city under a harsh dictatorship. It's quite a scary place to be, because anyone who steps out of line is for it—taken out by the secret police.

You are part of a group of people which has been following a great teacher who led a kind of religious revival—you had hoped he would over-throw the regime. To you and all of his followers, he was simply known as "the Master."

Of course, he had been closely watched by the secret police, as well as by the officials of the country who were collaborators. They were suspicious of anyone who had a following, and usually put down such people in order to keep control.

Until a few days ago, he had managed to avoid being captured. The secret police didn't want a public scene—they were afraid of rousing the support of the crowds for your leader, turning them in rebellion against the regime.

But one of the inner circle of his friends had turned out to be a double agent. While you were meeting and praying in a quiet place outside the city, he had led a group of secret police to where you were, and they had captured the Master.

Frightened out of your lives, and to your great shame, you all ran for cover. He was taken in and tortured, given a mockery of a trial, and then killed by the cruelest method the secret police could use.

Now you are in hiding in a safe house, along with others of his followers.

Imagine yourself there in an upstairs room in this house, on the third day after your leader was killed, terrified that every knock on the door will be the secret police. You do not know what your future will be, or even where your future will be. With the death of your leader, all hopes of a new order have gone.

Imagine your feelings—despair, disillusionment, fear, hopelessness, desperation. Where can you go? Is it safe to travel?

Two of your friends have fled from the city to their home in a village a few miles up the road. Another, Tom, has just popped home to make sure his wife and family are safe. The rest of you are feeling utterly lost and bewildered.

You are discussing some disturbing rumors, not knowing what to believe. One or two people, mainly women, claim to have seen the Master alive.

But that can't be possible; witnesses—including some of your number—saw him publicly executed. Others helped with his burial, and this was in a cave with a great stone in front and members of the elite guard to keep it secure.

So the story could well be a trap set by the secret police to get you all to break cover. You can't trust anyone in these times; you don't know who else might turn traitor.

Feel the fear and uncertainty.

While you are talking this over, the two who had headed out of the city turn up. You are surprised that they have dared to come back again.

They tell you the most amazing story. They claim that the Master, unrecognized, walked with them most of the way to the village, entrancing them with the way he talked about marvelous things—about himself and his destiny.

When they got home, they persuaded him to join them for a meal. They all sat down at the table, and he said the blessing over the bread as he *broke it. In that action they had instantly recognized him. To their amazement, it was the Master. At that moment he had disappeared from their sight, so they hurried back to the city.*

Well, that was a tall story, if ever there was one. Probably another secret police trap.

Yet surely these two couldn't have turned double agents as well? They're both very level-headed. So what are you to believe?

The next moment is one that will send shivers down your spine whenever you remember it. You are deep in discussion when suddenly, with no warning at all . . .

The Master is standing there in the middle of the room.

You are utterly devastated, shell-shocked. It is unbelievably terrifying.

He actually speaks some words, "May God's peace be with you"—just the sort of words he always used. You are all reacting in the same way. It's a ghost! It must be a ghost.

There's a kind of corporate gasp of terror, and you all draw back from him, petrified.

Everyone looks the way you feel—frightened, stupefied, desperately looking for an escape hatch but completely paralyzed, and unable to decide which way to turn.

More fear: he speaks again: "Why are you frightened?"

But you are—very frightened.

"It is really me," he says. "Look, you can see the marks of torture and execution on me. Why don't you touch me—a ghost doesn't have solid flesh and bones!"

You are in turmoil. Can he be real? If so, this is joy supreme.

Surely he's a ghost, an illusion, in which case this is terrifying.

Imagine your feelings, teetering between hope and terror.

He can see the doubts and fears mixed with joy in you all. And he speaks again.

"Have you got something to eat?" he says.

Someone hurriedly puts some of the supper on a plate and, gingerly, holds it out toward him.

There's a breathtaking silence as you watch, fascinated. What will happen?

He takes the plate, and then—to your amazement—he actually eats!

He is real.

You are completely overwhelmed; bursting with joy and wonder.

Can it be true? The Master, who was dead, very dead, is incredibly alive and well.

The world will never be the same again.

Imagine the excitement, the jubilation you all share, and will share forever.

Bask for a time in the blissful joy of knowing that he is alive and real.

Debriefing/Reflection

How do you respond to the fact of Jesus being physically alive? Not just spiritually alive, but real in flesh and bone.

Are you able to experience the joy, the excitement and the wonder of Jesus Christ alive, risen from the dead?

Are you able to worship him? To relate to him? To bring to him your thoughts, your prayers, your worries, your love and devotion?

What difference does Jesus alive make in your life?

PART TWO

OBEDIENCE AND DISCIPLESHIP

When my will is turned to Jesus
When obedience I employ
Then I know my Savior's promise
Of his gift of joy
When my thoughts are turned to Jesus
When my fears find true release
Then I know my Savior's promise
Of his gift of peace.

—Susie Hare, "When My Heart Is Turned"

11. MADE NEW

JOHN 3:1-10

One of the members of the Council* wanted to find out a bit more about Jesus. Perhaps he was shy of being criticized by the others, so he came to see Jesus by a back door after dark. And perhaps he thought a little flattery would get him a long way, because he started by saying how he thought Jesus must have come from God or he wouldn't have been able to heal sick people.

The response he got from Jesus must have been quite unexpected. Jesus said, "No one can set the Kingdom of God unless they are born anew."

Nicodemus (that was his name) was dumbfounded.

"You can't be," he said. "How can anyone be born, having grown old?"

Truth was, he probably didn't know what to say. This was way beyond him. Jesus was talking of a new kind of birth, a different kind.

Jesus explained more to Nicodemus. "In all truth, you cannot enter the Kingdom of God without being born of the Spirit. You have a human birth, and that makes you human. There is also a birth in the Spirit, which is what gives you spiritual life. It's not physical; just like the wind blows, you can't see it but you can hear it and feel it. That's what it's like being reborn in the Spirit."

Nicodemus had still not fully understood, because he expressed his incredulity.

"How can these things be?" he said.

But his life was affected because we hear of him again later in John's Gospel (John 19:38-42).

*The Council, or Sanhedrin, was a judicial body and in full was composed of some seventy-one members. It was dominated by the Sadducees, priestly, wealthy, and conservative; but it also included Pharisees, the strictest observers of the Law, of whom Nicodemus was one; and also laypeople.

Meditation

You are Nicodemus, a Pharisee and a member of the Council. You have become aware of Jesus and you are very interested in who he is and what he is doing.

You hear about him from various people. He has been preaching to crowds up and down the country. Many are talking about him, about the freshness and power of his teaching, about how he is proclaiming his Kingdom, and especially about the healing of sick people.

What does he mean by talking about his Kingdom?
He seems a puzzling person, yet he clearly has power and authority which must come from God, since he has healed many sick people.

All this has aroused in you more than curiosity, rather a deep longing, as though questions that have been nagging at you may have an answer in him.
Questions such as: what is this life really for? If our end is some greater life beyond the grave, then what is the way to this greater life? Is this new kind of life something to do with the Kingdom he talks about?
So you are searching intensely for something, although you don't know what.

Try to feel the emptiness and the curiosity that Nicodemus feels.
Feel the thirst for something to fill the gaps in your life.

You have held back from approaching Jesus.
As a Pharisee, you are strictly committed to keeping the Jewish Law. You are also aware that members of the Council are beginning to show concern about Jesus. The Sadducees in particular would rather like to have him out of the way; they really don't like any kind of threat to their authority.
So you dare not approach him openly, since you would put your position on the Council at risk.

Eventually you find out from one of his followers where he is staying, and you arrange to visit him late one evening.
As you come into the house, you have a sense of excitement, and also some hesitancy.
Where will you start? How can you form a question from what is deep down in your heart? Will Jesus be able to respond to your intense inner searching?

Jesus greets you. "Welcome," he says.
After a tongue-tied moment you blurt out a sentence. "Master," you say, "we know you are a Teacher from God. No one can do the miracles you do unless God is with him."

You are stunned by Jesus' reply. "The only way you can come within God's Kingdom is to be born again!"

You can't think what he's talking about. It seems an impossibility. You don't want to disagree directly with him, so, like the Pharisee you are, you put your disagreement as a question.
   "How can someone be born when they've already grown up? Surely they can't re-enter their mother's womb and be born."
   Jesus responds, "You are born once of human parents and that makes you human. But you need to be made new, to be reborn, and that is the work of the Holy Spirit. He is God at work. You can't see or touch or feel him, but you can become aware of the powerful effects he has. Like the wind—you can't see it but when it blows you can feel the force of it. When you respond to the power of the Holy Spirit, allowing yourself to be born again, you will soon know he is at work in you."

Still you find this impossible to understand. It is all very humbling.
   "How can these things be?" you say, really thinking aloud.

Imagine how you feel: you are a teacher of religious truth, a person in authority, yet you are unable to comprehend what this teacher is telling you.
   Reflect for a moment on the difficulty of grasping this revelation.

Now come to Jesus as yourself.
   Bring to Jesus the longings that are in your own life.
   What are they? Do you thirst for him to come into your life, to renew his life in you?
   Is there a yearning, an ache for something which is more than you already have in the faith?
   Bring all this to Jesus, and offer your needs, your longings to him.
   Hear him as he says to you, "You must be born anew in the Holy Spirit."
   Open your heart to God, asking that his Holy Spirit may live and grow in you.

Debriefing/Reflection

Are you able to identify needs and longings, empty spaces in your life?
   God the Holy Spirit is always at work in you, as you let him; you can ask him afresh to work in you, for his lifetime work in us is our growth into the person God has made us to be.

We sometimes think in terms of our *possessing* the Holy Spirit, forgetting that God gives him to us in order that God may work in us and through us. Marian Bushill, in *Seed Thoughts for Daily Meditation,* puts it well:

> We shall cease to think of getting possession of God's power and using it, but rather we shall think of the Spirit of power taking possession of us and using us.

How have you experienced the Holy Spirit taking possession of you and using you?

12. LOVING OBEDIENCE

LUKE 1:26-38

A young girl called Mary had a cousin, Elizabeth, who had miraculously conceived a child at quite an advanced age—after many years of praying and yearning. She was, of course, thrilled. But six months later an even more extraordinary thing happened to Mary, who was engaged to be married. She had a visit from an angel; well, not just any angel, an archangel—*the* archangel, Gabriel. It was a terrifying experience.

Mary was startled, bewildered, and awestruck.

After greeting her as one highly favored by God, and calming her fear, Gabriel dropped the bombshell: she was going to have a baby!

"Impossible," she said, "I'm a virgin—not even married yet."

Gabriel explained that this would be no ordinary baby; the conception was by the power of God the Holy Spirit. The child would be holy, and would be the Son of God.

Now Mary had a choice. She could say Yes, and go through severe trauma and grief (how *do* you explain to your fiancé that you are pregnant, but that you have not been unfaithful?)—the potential for complications was endless. Daunting.

Or maybe it would be simpler just to turn the whole thing down, and say a very firm No. Quite an attractive option. She could then go ahead with a normal married life, have children by Joseph, who had a decent trade, and they'd have a comfortable life. Much easier to say, No!

Mary was a devout servant of God. Her example of obedience to God and compliance with his will is immortalized in her response. Mary simply said, "Yes, I am God's handmaid, I will obey his will." So she went ahead, and had the baby, the Christ, Immanuel, God with us.

Meditation

You are in a dream but, as in many dreams, you can make decisions, and opt out if you really want to.

You are young and strong. And you are high up in the mountains. Picture yourself, at a level place, surrounded by snow-covered peaks, a huge wilderness of rock and ice, peak beyond peak, as far as you can see.

Although you are well clothed, it is biting cold at this altitude, and the keen wind freezes your face.

Many hundreds of feet below is the valley, with a stream of snow-melt rushing along, green at the edges, with fir trees scrambling a short way up the valley sides.

You are standing looking at this mixture of grandeur and bleakness, when a stranger comes toward you. A bit unexpected, as you had no idea any-one else was around.

No ordinary person, he is very tall and he has a kind of transparency as if he is a source of light, as if he has some special power, though what this is lies beyond your understanding.

Wondering, you watch him come nearer, and you see he is carrying some-thing, a bundle of something. Does he speak English, you wonder, or some other language?

He speaks, and you feel relieved that you can understand.

"Greetings." His voice has an unearthly sound—as though he were in an echoing cathedral.

"I have a message for you, and a request in the name of the living God."

So he must be an angel. And now you see that the bundle in his arms is a young child, a boy. He seems to be asleep, but he looks about eighteen months old.

"The message is this," he says. "You have been chosen by God for a mis-sion, a difficult task."

By now, you are more than a little frightened, and certainly wary. Excuses rise up in your mind, escape clauses. Maybe you are needed some-where else. You are expected back in the valley.

Imagine your feelings. What are they? Fear? Puzzlement? Awe? Perhaps also a sense of honor at having been chosen.

You try to be brave, and ask about the task. The child is needed, appar-ently, and expected by the people who live in a village some distance away.

The route is a tortuous one, a narrow path along the mountainside—you hadn't noticed it until he pointed it out.

Oh dear! Not a path you would choose. Picture it winding away, tucked into the mountainside, the sheer wall rising to one side, and a fearsome drop on the other straight down to the valley bottom. Dangerous.

You don't seem to know how far it would be or how long it would take. It is clear that the decision must be made. Now.

You have a choice; but how can you say No? God has asked you; the people seem to have been waiting and expecting this child for a long time. The child is an unknown quantity, but perhaps there is a parent waiting for him, or people are expecting him for some reason.

It will be a demanding task and an awesome responsibility. How do you feel about your response?

If you say, No, the dream ends, and you will wake up, a bit like ending a nightmare.

But if you choose to undertake the task, the dream goes on.

"Yes," you say. "If that is what God wills, yes. I will be his servant."

You pick up your pack from the ground, and put it on, and take the child from the angel. He is a very beautiful child, still asleep and not as heavy as you expected.

And you set out, feeling very unsure about the journey, or what it is you've undertaken, but glad you are obeying God's will.

The angel calls after you, "You will be given strength in time of need. God's grace will be enough."

You feel encouragement and hope.

As you step onto the path, the first waves of fear hit you. It's even narrower than you thought, more of a ledge than a path. Though you dare not look down, you are aware of the terrifying drop at your side, and the awesome responsibility of getting the child safely to the people awaiting him.

Imagine your feelings. What are they?

As you round the first bend, the path looks as though it winds on for miles. Worse, the valley seems to have dropped even lower, while the path climbs higher.

On the other hand, the child, now awake, smiles. It feels like gratitude; your heart warms to him. You feel that you must succeed in the journey.

You trudge on, hoping to make it to the village before nightfall; how will you cope if it gets dark early?

In some places rocks have fallen onto the path and they make the going harder. Now and then you hear a rock crashing down from the mountain above, sometimes ahead, sometimes behind, but always making a sickening, crunching noise.

Time seems to stop when they bounce off the path and you wait for the faint crash as they land on the rocks miles below.

You pray for strength.
And you sense God's grace helping you.

The child is getting heavier. But a bond is growing between you. He seems unconcerned at being carried by a stranger, but his weight is growing.
Worse, the mist is rising from below. While it hides the awful drop, the unknown distance below makes the danger feel worse.

Panic begins to set in. You pause for a moment to rest against the rock wall behind. What have you let yourself in for? Feel the fear beginning to haunt you.
"Lord, help me," you pray. "Lord, give me strength to go on."
You believe that God is with you even though you can't sense his presence.

Time to move on. Your arms and back are aching, but the child seems to radiate something that feels like love.
You must keep going. Dusk is beginning to fall, and there is no sign of the village.

Ahead, the path seems to disappear, and a fresh wave of fear hits you.
Then you realize: the track is going through a sort of tunnel. A relief from the frightful drop to your side, but you have to feel your way through the dark, one hand on the rock wall, the other taking the growing weight of the child.

Just when you are getting used to it, your hand is leaning against thin air; you stumble and almost trip.
You stop again to get your bearings and see where you are.
The path just winds on. Surely you will come to the village soon.

The child is heavier still, but he smiles at you and you feel encouraged. He is very beautiful and somehow you know he is very precious.
In face, grace and power radiate from him, and you feel yourself gaining courage and strength.

Now as you look ahead you can see what must be the lights of the village twinkling in the distance.
You brace herself and push on, but taking care now as the dusk is making it ever harder to see.

As the village gets closer, the child seems almost unbearably heavy. You stumble on.

Now you can see people with flaming torches, a sort of welcome. Relief mixes with the fatigue as you push on, very cautiously, for the last half mile.

At last you reach the end of that fearful path, and the villagers greet you and the child. There is great rejoicing.

Stumbling with exhaustion, you allow them to lead you to a sort of barn, where there is a place to put the child down. Someone brings food for the child and for you.

You have made it. You are overwhelmed with joy, relief, and utter weariness.

You learn of the long years that they have waited for this child (though, strangely, some seem disappointed; they expected someone grander).

Visitors come to admire him. Important people come and bring him strange gifts, and talk of his future. You are dazed by it all.

Suddenly you are aware of the angel (though no one else seems to see him).

The angel says to you, "Well done, you good and faithful servant." He also warns of hard times ahead—for it seems your task has only just begun.

However, you will face whatever comes now, for you have learned the rewards of obedience to God's loving will.

"Well done, good servant," he says, "you have brought the Christ Child to his people."

Debriefing/Reflection

How did you make your decision? And how did you feel about it?

When have you ever experienced a call from God, a requirement to fulfill a task that seems too great? And in accepting that task, have you found God's strength—his grace—sufficient to enable you to complete it?

What have you learned from the example of Mary's obedience?

God opens up opportunities to serve him in all kinds of ways. Usually these are in seemingly small things—a helping hand, a thoughtful word, a listening ear. Often they come to you in quite unexpected ways. Think of examples, and how you have responded.

13. IN MY HEART

LUKE 2:22-35

In all Jewish families, the firstborn child was symbolically given to God as an offering in memory of the time when the whole nation of Israel escaped from Egypt hundreds of years earlier. So Jesus was taken to the temple in Jerusalem to be presented to God by Mary and Joseph.

They were also bound by Jewish law to make an offering for purification after childbirth (a reflection of the thinking of those times). The offering would have been a pair of turtledoves or two young pigeons.

While they were there, a very interesting person visited the temple, led by the Spirit. His name was Simeon; he was old and had been promised by God that he would not die until he had seen the Messiah. Guided by the Holy Spirit, he came to the temple when Mary and Joseph were there with Jesus. He recognized Jesus instantly, took him into his arms and praised God with some words which have become famous: "Lord, now you are letting your servant go in peace as you have promised, for my eyes have seen your salvation . . . "

Joseph and Mary were amazed at what was being said, but Simeon blessed them and said to Mary. "This child is destined for the fall and rise of many in Israel, and to be a sign that will be opposed so that the inner thoughts of many will be revealed—and a sword will pierce your own soul too."

Meditation

Imagine yourself at the temple in Jerusalem. It is a magnificent building on a huge site—nearly one-fifth of the city—and around are splendid colonnades.

You are spending some time in the temple to worship God and to pray to him, to be still and to be close to him.

You find great peace in this place, with its history of holiness and its breathing of God's nearness.

Feel the sense of awe in his presence.

As you come to the end of your time of prayer, a couple enter with their child to make the offering for purification—in their case two pigeons, the offering made by poor people.

Nothing unusual in that; people come and go all the time to make such offerings, and you assume that their son is the firstborn, brought to be presented to God.

Shortly after them an old man comes in. You recognize him as Simeon, a devout man and a prophet. You have seen him many times before in the temple.
   He is clearly full of great joy to see this couple and especially their child.
   You look on with great interest as he approaches the family.

To your surprise he takes the child into his arms. And in a voice like a chant he proclaims some words, words as a prophet would speak, with his face uplifted to heaven.
   "Lord God," he chants, "your servant can now leave this world in peace.
   My eyes have seen the long-awaited Messiah, the Christ of God.
   He is the salvation for your people, and a light to the world,
   The glory of your people."

You are astonished. This is extraordinary; can the child really be the promised Christ?
   Then you look at the parents' faces—they too are overwhelmed with surprise.
   "What's going on?" you whisper to the person nearest to you.
   They seem to know the parents, Joseph and Mary, and their history. They explain that the child was born nearby in Bethlehem, and that shepherds and wise men had come to worship, having learned of his birth in visions. It had been revealed to them that the child was the Christ.

You are still amazed. This is so unexpected; its significance is quite staggering.

There is more. Simeon is speaking again. This time he is specifically addressing the mother of the child, Mary.
   Something about the rise and fall of people, and the revealing of inner thoughts. You are so surprised that you are not really taking it all in.

But then you are startled by some words he says to Mary: ". . . and a sword shall pierce your own soul too."
   You start to ponder the meaning of this strange saying. A sword piercing her soul? What can he possibly mean by that?
   She looks to you like an innocent young mother. Surely the mother of the Christ would be held in great honor. How can being the mother of the Christ really be like a sword in the soul?

As you wonder, you find yourself losing consciousness of the present; a vision gradually comes into focus.

A scene unfolds. You see Mary and Joseph in Jerusalem again. Their son is growing up, about twelve years old, and they are just leaving the city at the end of the annual Passover festival.

You see them walking on the long journey home in a party of family and friends. They are chatting happily to their companions as they come to a halt for the night. They look around, and then start searching.

The worry on their faces changes to horror; they have lost their son, Jesus. He's not in the party.

You see them turn back hurriedly to Jerusalem. They search the city desperately for him, looking in all the possible places for three long days.

Then at last they see him. He's sitting with a group of the men of learning, teachers, listening to them, discussing, asking them questions. The wise old men are staggered by his insight and understanding.

You see the look on their faces, and share their wonder.

His parents are very distressed. His mother says, "How could you treat us like this? We've been looking for you everywhere, sick with worry."

And their son, so young, says something which makes you marvel even more. "Why were you searching for me? Didn't you know that I must be about the work of my heavenly Father?"

The remarkable thing is that Mary doesn't disagree. She doesn't understand, but accepts this with the same obedience to God as when she accepted being the mother of the Messiah—accepts that he has to fulfill a God-given destiny.

You feel for Mary as you begin to perceive the cost of being mother to the Christ.

The scene moves on. Joseph dies—he was much older than Mary—so Mary carries the burden of being the mother of the Messiah on her own.

When he is fully mature, Jesus sets out from home and starts to preach the Kingdom of God.

You look on as Mary sees him draw followers about him; she sees him travel far, suffer hunger, heat, and cold.

She sees him loving and caring for people; healing the sick, giving sight to the blind, feeding the hungry.

She also sees opposition to him grow among the officials, and she hears the threats to his life. You become aware of her fear—she is afraid of the danger to him.

She nurtures him as she can. But she cannot stop him from following God's chosen path, or prevent his enemies from taking him prisoner.

Again you sense the cost to Mary. You had thought that the Christ, as a king, would overcome all opposition.

But then in your vision you see great cruelty; Jesus is condemned to suffer a hideous death on a cross.

And you see Mary torn by grief nearby. You see her terrible anguish as she watches her son die. Surely this is the sword which pierces her soul.

How, you wonder, can she possibly bear this?

The pain of watching a loved one suffer is so much greater than one's own pain. And what appalling suffering this is. For Jesus a horrific death; for Mary the long drawn out agony of his suffering.

You admire the wonderful loyalty and obedience she demonstrates.

You marvel as you perceive the way in which Jesus both gives and draws to himself love and loyalty.

In your vision you sense that God is working something out in this death, but your own sight is too blurred to understand.

You had thought that the Christ would be more like a successor to David, a king and a warrior. Jesus is utterly different; and Mary his mother reflects this in her life—goodness, gentleness, compassion, and great joy.

As the vision gradually fades, you feel a sense of tremendous privilege at the insight you, a mere onlooker, have been granted.

You look again at this mother and her son in the temple. You reflect on the qualities she shows, and on this Christ who generates love and devotion of this order.

Can you too become like her, obedient to God?

Can you reflect, as she does, his love and goodness?

Can you bear, as she does, the costly suffering of discipleship?

73

Debriefing/Reflection

Mary has been called "the selfless space in which God became man . . . the silence in which his Word can be heard" (Margaret Magdalen, *Jesus— Man of Prayer,* Eagle, p. 85). How can we fulfill this role?

Can we bear the cost of discipleship as Mary did? Can we forgive people who hurt those we love?

What is it about Jesus that draws from us the same obedience, loyalty, and love?

14. One Thing Is Required

MATTHEW 4:18-22; MARK 10:17-22

Early in his ministry, Jesus chose some people to work with him, to be his disciples. The first of these were working as fishermen on the Sea of Galilee. One day, as they were at work, he just said to them, "Follow me and I will make you fishers of people." They immediately left their work at the nets and went with him—Simon Peter and his brother Andrew, and two other brothers, James and John.

Later he called more people to join him.

Over the next two or three years they learned a vast amount from Jesus and about Jesus. They witnessed wonderful things—healing and forgiveness. Many things stuck in their minds. One of these was what happened when a young man came to Jesus asking for guidance to achieve eternal life. Jesus asked him about the way in which he was keeping the Jewish Law. He responded that he had carefully kept to the Law since his early youth. Eagerly, he asked, "What more must I do?"

Jesus looked at him with love and said, "There is just one thing you have missed out. Go and sell all that you have, give the money to the poor, and then come and follow me." This shocked the young man, and he went away with great sadness because he had many possessions.

Later Jesus said something to his disciples which they would only fully understand after his death and resurrection. He said, "If anyone wants to be one of my followers, let them deny themselves and take up their cross daily and follow me."

Meditation

You are a fisherman, one of a group that works on the Sea of Galilee. You can choose the name of one of the four disciples (Simon, Andrew, James, or John), or simply use your own name.

It's quite a hard life, but you enjoy the water, the boats, the open air, and the comradeship of working with the others.

Imagine a day when the big lake is brightly lit by the morning sun, the boats hauled up on the beach. You are busy spreading out the nets to dry, ready for another night's fishing.

All is well. Sense the contentment and peace of the morning. Enjoy the scene.

Now a stranger comes walking in your direction. You don't see many strangers on the beach. For some reason he seems impressive, has an air of authority, of one who clearly knows what he is doing and where he is going.

Perhaps he is the person who, so you heard, stood up in the synagogue last Sabbath and read from the prophet Isaiah. He had declared on that occasion that the prophecy was fulfilled in himself, God's anointed one.

You all stand looking at him with interest and curiosity as he comes toward you.

You sense, but you cannot explain, an air of great power and authority in him and a wonderful attractiveness.

He somehow calls forth immediate respect, even though he hasn't spoken.

When he does speak, you all get a surprise. No greeting, no formalities, simply the words, "Follow me, and I will make you fish for people."

Those words carry a depth of meaning. Not just "walk behind me" or "walk with me." Rather something like: "Come and be one of my people, a friend, a disciple. Come and share in a great task, a worthwhile quest. Come and share the risks and dangers; share the joys and the fruits."

His call is not irresistible, but his authority and his charisma are so attractive that you and the others leave your nets just as they are, and go with him.

See yourself now embarking on an adventure and an endeavor of immense proportions. Your life is filled with events and with growth as you learn from Jesus.

The days and weeks seem a whirl of crowds, miracles, healings, sermons, journeys.

At the heart of the activity is Jesus, teaching you and showing you new insights—about God, about his Kingdom, about forgiveness, compassion, and prayer.

Your life, your being, are changing from the inside.

You find yourself growing ever more at one with Jesus and the other disciples as he teaches you about himself.

Gradually you come to believe that he is truly the Son of God, as he says of himself.

You are in awe of his power, his compassion and his attractive goodness.

Others join you. Not all stay, for some cannot believe Jesus, or don't want to believe him. But you find yourself committed to this new kind of journey in the company of Jesus.

One young man leaves an impression. He is full of enthusiasm, and comes running to Jesus.

"Master," he says, "I too would like to achieve the eternal life you speak of. What must I do?"

Surely, you think, this man would be an ardent follower and disciple. He's enthusiastic and seems inspired. He's also very well dressed—must be quite wealthy.

Jesus sees into people's hearts, and takes them forward one step at a time.

"Well," he says, "the first thing is to be sure you can keep to the Jewish Law, the commandments of God. Have you been true in keeping the Law?"

"Oh yes," says the young man. "I have kept the Law in every detail very carefully from the time I was old enough to understand. But is there more I can do? What else is required of me?"

"That's good," Jesus says, "that you keep the Law." You see him looking with love at the young man, and seeing deep into his heart.

"Just one thing more is required. Go and sell all your possessions, everything you own. Then give the money to poor people, and come and follow me."

Now, you think, that is tough, harsh even. Jesus has never told the rest of you to sell your possessions. You wonder how the young man will react.

But you don't have to wait long. He looks utterly crestfallen and you realize that he can't face the cost of this kind of discipleship—he's too attached to what he possesses. Or maybe they really possess him.

He goes away, and you feel sad for him.

Later Jesus really sets you thinking, "Anyone who wants to follow my Way," he says, "must deny the self, and take up their cross daily and follow me."

You pause to reflect on this—the cost of letting go and releasing the hold that self and possessions have on you. It's actually like being crucified so that the selfish person in me dies.

Now move the scene to the present day. Imagine you are in your home.

Jesus comes to see you. He wants you to be his follower, his disciple, to walk with him, to experience the joy of life shared with him, to brave its ups and downs.

But first he looks deep into your heart, and he asks you, "What is most important in your life? What one possession or what one activity matters more than anything else in the world? What would you least like to let go of?"

He asks you to think deeply to identify this one thing—but note, it is not likely to be a person except in an inappropriate relationship, because he knows that true love of another person should be a reflection of his love.

So what holds you more than anything else? Is it something precious that you own? Or is it something you enjoy doing more than anything else?

While you are thinking, Jesus is standing in the doorway, waiting for you. He will never force you, there is no compulsion, but he is offering you discipleship, a life journey with him.

When you have found that one thing—or it may be more than one—try to hand it over to Jesus, give it to him as a present. Release your ownership, and let him release any hold it has on you.

Then let him take you by the hand and walk with him, rejoicing in his company.

Allow the joy of his freedom to take hold of you.

Debriefing/Reflection

Were you able to identify and release to Jesus anything which might possibly possess you rather than Jesus?

What does discipleship mean to you?

In the New Testament it meant mainly one who was a pupil of a Rabbi or master, but you could discuss how Jesus gave the term a wider meaning.

15. Your Hand Outstretched

MATTHEW 14:22-33

Afterone of those really busy days, Jesus got his disciples to take themselves in a boat across the lake, while he went up into the hills alone, as he so often did, to pray. That evening, those in the boat were a good way from the shore, but struggling against a strong wind.

They must have struggled for a long while because as daylight was beginning to break, Jesus came to them, walking on the water. They were terrified—they thought they were seeing a ghost. They were certainly shouting out with fear. But Jesus immediately calmed them, saying, "Take heart, it is I. There's no need to be afraid."

So they calmed down. Peter was, as always, adventurous and perhaps excited by seeing Jesus. He said, "If it is you, then, command me to come to you over the water."

Jesus answered him, "Come to me."

So Peter stepped out of the boat and began walking toward Jesus over the water. All was fine until he noticed how strong the wind was, and how big the waves were. Then he became frightened and began to sink.

He called out to Jesus, "Help, Lord. Save me!" Jesus reached out a hand, caught him, and held him firmly. But he also said to Peter, "What little faith you have. Why did you doubt me?"

They got to the boat and the wind died down. The disciples were overawed and worshiped Jesus, saying, "Truly you are the Son of God."

Meditation

Imagine that you and some friends have decided late one summer evening to row across a large lake. It could be in the Great Lakes region, or perhaps a lake in Louisiana. It's a big lake, and there are five or six of you in a heavy rowing boat.

Picture yourself, then in the boat with your friends. You all get on very well and it's good to be with them. Because of the distance, you are going to take it in turns to row. It seems quite an adventure and you are all bubbling with exhilaration.

The surroundings are beautiful. You can see trees and hills.

The daylight has lasted very late, but the first stars are beginning to appear. The air is fresh and clean, and you find it all very agreeable.

You're happy to take your turn on the oars.

What none if you had bargained for was the wind, which has now got up and is blowing quite strongly.

Pulling on the oars is becoming very hard work; in fact, your arms are aching and you are panting with the effort. You wonder if that boat is moving forward at all or whether it is just going backward.

Your feelings are now changing. What was a pleasing outing is gradually becoming less pleasant and rather worrying.

Imagine the fears that are welling up in you.

You feel relieved when someone else offers to take a turn with the oars.

Night has closed in, and you can barely see a distant outline of land. You wonder whether you are even heading in the right direction.

In spite of all your efforts, you find yourself shivering as you wrap your coat tightly around you and hunch rather miserably in a corner of the seat at the stern.

Your friends have fallen silent now after some murmurs of concern, all wrapped in their own thoughts.

Imagine your feelings as you peer into the night trying to see a familiar landmark; and then huddle into your coat to shut out the chill.

You must have dozed for quite a long while because the first glimmers of daylight are dispersing the dark of the short summer night. The wind is still blowing hard, and someone is struggling with the oars.

You feel even colder. The shore seems no nearer and you shut your eyes again—perhaps to hide from the reality.

The others are looking around for familiar signs. Suddenly you hear a concerted intake of breath. Then a gasp of horror.

You open your eyes.

You find yourself screaming with fear. There is someone, a ghost, walking on the water not far from the boat, and coming toward you.

You are terrified. Whatever can it be?

In a moment's pause a voice, which you feel sure you know, speaks. "It's all right, it's me, Jesus. You don't need to be afraid."

Your terror gives way to a whirlpool of feelings—joy, excitement, wonder. Can it be true? you think. How can he be walking on the water?

Can it really be Jesus coming to us?

You look at him. He is strong, brings great assurance and comfort. He has never let you down.

An impulse takes you. I want to go to him, you think, I would really like to be with him. I wonder how . . .

Without thinking, you blurt out, "Lord, if it's really you can I come to you?"

Immediately Jesus says, "Yes, come on, come to me."

You don't hesitate; you stand up, put one foot over the side of the boat, and test what is there.

Your foot seems to be supported. You don't look down but keep your eyes on Jesus.

Gingerly you put your weight on that foot and bring the other leg over the side of the boat. Still looking at Jesus, you let go of the boat, and now you are fully supported by the water.

It feels like walking on a very delicate membrane. It feels as though it's moving a little, but not enough to throw you off your balance.

You feel it's rather exciting.

You put one foot in front of the other and tentatively step toward Jesus, keeping your eyes on him. You find yourself holding your arms out on either side like a tightrope walker.

You walk some more steps. You feel wonderfully exhilarated.

You can hardly believe you are actually walking on the water, and going to meet Jesus.

You are tempted to look around at the others, as much as to say "Look at me then." But you know you must keep your eyes on Jesus.

Another step or two, and you will be nearly there.

You wonder why the waves are not making you wet—they are quite large.

And what happened to the wind? It was blowing so strongly before.

It's blowing still. In that moment you become very aware of just how strong it is. And the waves, they're quite big too. And noisy. Frightening.

In that moment you have taken your eyes off Jesus and become first aware, and then overwhelmed by the power of the wind and waves. They dominate your surroundings, and they make you feel small and defenseless.

Confidence evaporates and you find yourself surrendering to a kind of helpless despair, giving in to the forces of wind and wave.

The support under your feet is going. You can't be sinking, surely?
You try to make your feet climb upward, but still you are sinking. You are going down and down into the waves, overcome by their power.

Terrified, panic-stricken, you cry out, "Jesus, help me! Save me!"
Immediately a strong hand outstretched grasps your hand. You are held and supported.
You find yourself with Jesus back above the waves, secure, safely held by his hand. Very gently Jesus says to you, "What happened to your faith? Perhaps you took your eyes off me."

You are quickly back at the boat, and you are suddenly aware that the wind and waves have dropped completely.
The morning sun is warming you. You are warmed more by Jesus, his wonderful power.
And you reflect: how could I have taken my eyes off him? Could I really have thought the wind and waves were more powerful?

You have had a marvelous experience, walking on water; but a still greater experience of his supporting strength.
You bask in his presence, and try to resolve always to trust him.

Debriefing/Reflection

Many things come and hit us during our lives: illness, painful events. Think of examples. Sometimes they threaten to sink us.

How can we respond to such events by trusting in Jesus, having total faith in him?

What prayers and psalms and Bible passages will help to support us?

What is your experience of sinking, and then turning to Jesus for help, and finding his hand outstretched?

16. Trust Like a Child

LUKE 7:28-35; MARK 10:13-16

When John the Baptist sent disciples to Jesus to check whether he was indeed the one who was expected or whether they should be looking elsewhere, Jesus gave a very clear message by showing all the signs which demonstrated that he was the expected Messiah—the blind could see, the lame could walk, the sick were healed, the gospel was being preached.

He went on to talk about John—the messenger, and a great man. He also upbraided those who would not listen to John, especially some of the hypocritical leaders such as the Pharisees. And when Jesus came preaching in a different style, they wouldn't listen to him either. He likened them to children playing in the marketplace who were choosy about which games they joined in.

At one time when he was teaching, people brought young children to him, asking for a blessing. The disciples tried to turn the people away. But Jesus, quite indignant, said, "Let the children come to me, and don't stop them. God's kingdom belongs to such little ones. Indeed, you won't get near the kingdom unless you develop a childlike trust and faith."

And Jesus put his arms around them and blessed them.

Meditation

You are the parent of young children, and you live in a town in Judea. You and other parents sometimes join together and bring your children to spaces where they can play—either outside the town or in the marketplace when it's not too busy.

Picture the scene in the marketplace one sunny morning. You are four adults enjoying chatting together, and ten children aged between four and eight years old at play.

There's plenty of space today. No one seems to be selling animals or fruit and vegetables or other wares. There's one of those traveling preachers in the far corner, who seems to have attracted quite a few people.

You sit together on a stone bench while the children decide what games to play. It's very pleasant.

The children all get on so well together and enjoy playing; the older ones are so good with the younger ones.

However, today the children have become unusually fractious. They argue about which game to play. Voices are raised.
    "No, I don't want to play that game. It's silly."
    "Well, I don't want to play your game. It's boring."
    And, like children the world over, they squabble on and on, and eventually they choose a game—though some with bad grace.

The game is called "imitations." One half choose an activity which mimics the way adults behave and the rest guess and join in.
    Usually there is a great deal of laughter, because some adult behavior seems quite ridiculous to children, and the standard jokes are often repeated.

You have half an ear to the game as you chat to the other adults, while the children make their first choice. Ironically they've chosen adults chatting together—probably thinking of you.
    The choosers lead the others. "Talk, talk, talk, talk," they cry.
    And the rest all join in, shouting, "Chatter, chatter, chatter, chatter!" until they all collapse in laughter.

The next imitation is dancing. The choosers pretend to make music on pipes, shouting as if to a tune, "Pipe, pipe, pipe, pipe," and the others are meant to join in dancing.
    But this time the others are perverse and won't dance. The choosers are despondent. They grumble and complain.
    You have stopped chatting and feel involved with the children in their game, saddened at the unaccustomed squabbling.

They decide to have one more try. This time it's mourning, which normally gets the most laughter.
    They wail and wail and wail, at which the others are meant to join in pretending to weep and weep.
    The five others are now totally stubborn, even surly. They start to complain to each other, and then fall silent.

Across the market square the preacher is still speaking, and in that rather ill-natured quietness you can now hear what he is saying.
    "People of today have shut their ears to hearing the truth from God, no matter how the message is delivered.
    "John the Baptist came and was frugal but you didn't want to hear him.

84

"The Son of Man has come celebrating and preaching God's Kingdom of joy, but you won't hear him either."

The children are still silent, but the nature of the silence seems to have changed.

You are aware of a kind of respect, even reverence for this man who speaks like a prophet.

You wonder whether he means himself when he says "the Son of Man."

You find yourself responding too. He speaks with authority. His voice has a quality which resonates with all your deepest longings.

You focus more attention on him.

He has noticed the children's games and now uses them as an illustration.

"I'll tell you what it's like; it's like telling God's message of joy to people who don't want to hear.

"It's like children playing in the marketplace and saying to each other, 'We piped and you would not dance; we wailed and you did not weep'—that's the response to God's message of his Kingdom.' "

His effect, especially on the children, is remarkable. They look toward him, open-eyed, a new serenity possessing them. In fact they seem to be moving toward him.

He has a marvelous attraction, and you find yourselves standing up and moving across the square with the children, drawn by him, by a sense of his goodness and his power, and a yearning to know more.

One of the parents says, "He must be truly great. Surely he's a prophet from God. Let's ask him to bless the children—he is having such a miraculous effect on them."

You agree. You feel that here is someone exceptional, holy. His blessing on the children would be a blessing indeed.

You take the children by the hand to lead them to him, and they come with willingness. They still look toward him, but the people standing around block their vision and the way through to him.

You start to ask people to let you through, and they begin to stand aside.

But some of his friends stop you. "Hush," they say, "you can't interrupt him. People want to hear what he says."

This is a harsh setback. Imagine your feelings, your hurt.

The children are hurt too at being blocked; they can't understand why they should not be allowed near to this special man who draws them.

But he has noticed—he seems aware of all that goes on around him.

"Don't stop them," he says with some indignation. "Don't stop them; let the children come to me. God loves them; his Kingdom belongs to these little ones."

You now lead the children to him. Closer, you have an even greater sense of both his power and his love. The children are awestruck.

He takes each child in turn, puts one arm around their shoulders, and with the other hand on their head he blesses them in the name of the living God.

Imagine your feelings, your emotions, as he blesses your children.

When he has blessed the last child, he stands her in front of him and says, "If you want to accept the kingdom of God, his rule in your hearts and lives, you need to be like this child. You must have faith and obedience which is like that of a child for a loving parent."

You reflect on this: faith like a child's in a loving parent.

Obedience to God's will like the loving response of a child to a loving parent.

You ask yourself: is my faith like that? Is my obedience to God of that order?

Perhaps you want to say something to Jesus. Or just stay in his presence, basking in his peace-giving love.

Debriefing/Reflection

What does a childlike faith mean to you?

Perhaps you would like to pray to God and ask his grace to help you to such faith and such obedience.

How do you see the difference between a childish faith and a childlike faith?

How can we develop a faith that is more childlike in trust and belief?

17. The Good Wine

JOHN 2:1-11

One day, Jesus and his disciples were invited to a wedding. His mother was there as well. They were all having a good time but, quite early on, the wine ran out. There must have been some concern because Jesus' mother came to him and told him that there was no wine. But Jesus said to her, "Woman (which was like saying "mother"), what concern is that to you and me? My hour has not yet come." Mary said to the servants, "Do whatever he tells you."

Jesus told them to fill the big stone jars with water. The Jews normally used these jars for ritual cleansing. So they filled them up to the brim.

Then Jesus told them to draw some out and take it to the chief steward of the feast—a sort of head waiter.

When the chief steward tasted the water which was now wine—but he didn't know where it came from—he was amazed at how good it was. He called the bridegroom to him and said, "Most people serve the best wine first, and when people have had plenty to drink they bring out the inferior wine. You have kept the good wine until now."

John calls this act the first of the "signs" which Jesus did in Galilee, revealing his glory.

Meditation

You are one of the followers of Jesus. Today is a day of some excitement because a friend of Jesus and his mother is getting married. They have both been invited to the wedding, and you have all been asked as well. Quite an honor.

The wedding goes off very well, and there is a great feast afterward, lasting a long time, with plenty to eat and drink. You are all thoroughly enjoying yourselves.

Picture yourself at the reception having a good time. The bride is beautiful and radiant. She and the bridegroom look blissfully happy.

Everyone around seems delighted for them both and for their families.

There seem to be a great many more guests than expected. You and the other close friends of Jesus add up to an extra twelve or more, and others seem to have come to join in the fun. The place certainly feels very crowded.

You are just thinking about this when there is a whisper of dismay. People are waving empty wine cups, and muttering that it was high time they had a refill.

The servants are agitated, rushing around with empty wine jugs. It very much looks as though they have run out of wine.

That's deeply embarrassing. You feel concern for the family. Important guests will be insulted and there'll be great shame for the bridegroom and his family if they can't find some more.

You look around to see who is near you. You see Jesus and, quite close to him, his mother. She is talking to him. "They've run out of wine," she says. "They're in great trouble. Can you help?"

Jesus seems to be stalling. "That's not really our concern at present," he says. "There will be a time and place for me to show God's glory."

You wonder what he means by that. Perhaps he is going to help solve the problem, but maybe he's not just digging people out of a hole.

It could be that he's also going to be saying something important by what he does. He's good at that.

Your intense curiosity is awakened.

You see Mary beckoning to one of the servants. "Whatever he tells you to do," she says, "just do it without question."

She clearly has great faith in him, and tries to convey this to the servants.

Jesus is looking toward the entrance to the courtyard, where there are some of those big water jars used for ritual cleansing.

"You see those stone jars," he says. "Go and fill them up with water."

You are watching the servants' faces—frowning with puzzlement and disbelief, as though they think Jesus is quite mad.

They hesitate, uncertain as to what they should do. But then they catch Mary's eye, apparently remember her instructions and reassurance, and go off to start drawing the water.

You become aware again of the mutterings around you which have become stronger, and are beginning to turn into complaint. And it is starting to be embarrassing. The atmosphere, at first so full of fun, is becoming sour.

You wonder what Jesus has in mind. He can't be expecting people to drink water—that would make matters very much worse.

You look across at the servants again. They're working as fast as they can, so they clearly have a sense of the urgency.
One of the other followers of Jesus catches your eye. He's as puzzled as you are. You shrug your shoulders and sigh as if to say, "I've no idea what's happening," and he opens his hands in a kind of despair.

One of the older servants comes rushing over to Jesus. "We've filled all the water jars," he says, panting hard.
"Very good," says Jesus. "Now start to draw from them with your wine jugs, and take it to the guests, starting with the chief steward."
There's another moment of disbelief and hesitation. Then he shrugs his shoulders and, with a look which says he's only doing this to humor Jesus, he collects the other servants together.
They gather up the jugs, and the one who had spoken to Jesus draws the first jugful from the water jar.

The look of sheer amazement on his face is something you will never forget. It is followed closely by a smile of great delight.
He looks at Jesus with awe and admiration in his eyes.
You wonder what that is all about.

He carries the jug to the chief steward, not far from you but with his back to the stone jars. Still smiling as the chief steward gratefully holds out his empty cup, the servant pours from the jug.
It's your turn to be amazed—the liquid is not water, but red like wine. And then you too are filled with delight. It is wine.
This is quite extraordinary; you are astounded at the power of Jesus.

You watch the chief steward as he takes first a sip, and then—a look of bliss on his face—he takes a gulp. And then another.
He laughs, and calls to the bridegroom. "Young man," he says, "this is remarkable. All the wedding feasts I've ever attended start off with the best wine. Then when we've had plenty to drink and won't notice what we're drinking, they bring out the poor stuff.
"But this is good wine you've brought out; it's magnificent. I'm most impressed."

The dour mutterings have disappeared, and cheerful conversation and laughter are bubbling back into the party. The atmosphere now has a greater sense of joy and delight than it did at the beginning.

You believe that Jesus is saying something through what he has done. John, who's close to him, would say it's a vision of his glory. That will take time to understand.

But you do know that he always creates fun and laughter and joy around him.

You remember how he quoted what they were saying about him. "John the Baptist came not eating and drinking, and they said he had a devil. The Son of Man comes, eating and drinking, and they call him a glutton and a drunkard."

You recall how he referred to himself as a kind of bridegroom, the one who arrives and brings joy and merriment. "You can't fast when the bridegroom is with you," he said. "The bridegroom is like new wine, good wine, a source of joy."

The festivities continue with great merrymaking. But you are still completely astounded by the wonder of this miracle of Jesus.

You are content to stand at one side and reflect on how this all came out of an act of faith in Jesus and obedience to his command. Such an unlikely command, yet obedience brought this flow of joy.

You take some time to think on this and absorb what it means.

Debriefing/Reflection

Have you experienced calling to God for help, and finding an unexpected answer? His answer is often a surprise.

How do you understand the idea of obedience? Obedience to God's commands, and to his will—even when they seem foolish?

How do you think that Jesus "revealed his glory" in this, the first of the "signs" in John's Gospel?

18. THE BLESSING

LUKE 19:29-38

Against all sensible advice, and in spite of threats, Jesus headed for Jerusalem at the time of the great Passover Festival. Instead of going in quietly by a back way, he chose to ride in state along the main highway from a neighboring village. Well, sort of in state. Not on a war-horse, but on a donkey (one which had never been ridden before) borrowed for the purpose. The Jews were expecting the Christ to come as a mighty king, a second David, but there was another prophecy in the scriptures that said, "Your king comes meek and riding upon an ass."

But the humble entry was turned into a triumph by the crowds, who made a kind of royal path, spreading cloaks and branches of palm pulled from the trees along the way. They made a lot of noise too, shouting, "Blessed is the King who comes in the name of the Lord! Hosanna to the Son of David!" So Jesus rode into Jerusalem as Messiah, Son of David, and royal king, humble yet triumphant.

Meditation

You are a market gardener growing fruit and vegetables for sale at the market in the city of Jerusalem, a mile away, more or less. You work very hard indeed, digging, hoeing, watering, and harvesting. You have a family of three young children, aged about four, six, and eight years old.

Picture your plot of land: at one edge is the small house, then there are rows of vegetables, some fruit bushes and trees. There's a good deep well—all important in the dry season.

Along one side runs the dusty track which leads to Jerusalem. It's rarely busy, but now and then useful for selling produce to travelers.

In a paddock near the house is your donkey. She is the means of transporting your goods to the market, strong enough to carry two big baskets laden with vegetables and fruit.

Now see yourself one hot and sunny afternoon, at work quite near the track. You are hoeing a fine row of vegetables, and in the next day or two you will harvest them and take them to the market, along with some fruit which is ready for picking.

You have a good crop which should enable you to buy extra food for your family, as well as oil for your lamps and other goods for your house.

The sun beats down, relentlessly. You are feeling the heat and, pausing to wipe away the sweat dripping into your eyes, you lean on the hoe for a minute or two to rest.

As you look up, to your great amazement—and concern—you see two men, strangers, at the edge of the track. They are untying your donkey who is, unusually, grazing at the entrance.

You hurry toward them, shouting, "Hey! What do you think you're doing? That's my donkey you are stealing."

"It's all right," one of them says, quite gently, "The Master has sent us to take her."

"What do you mean?" you say. "What Master is this? You can't take my donkey."

"The Master is a great and holy man," they say. "He comes from God. You are being asked to give your donkey to God, for him to use."

"Well," you say, rather more doubtfully, "if it's for God . . . but how am I to know?"

"We have been with him for three years," they say. "His name is Jesus, and he is a great prophet, full of God's power. He has healed many sick people—opened the eyes of the blind, made the mute to speak, and the lame to walk.

"He has done much good and no harm to anyone. I'm sure he will see you are all right, I promise you."

You hesitate. You still feel very uncertain, but if God is asking you, through these men, you must let your donkey go . . .

As they go off, leading her away, misgivings well up in your heart.

What if she doesn't come back? You will be lost without her. How will you manage?

See yourself standing there, all anxiety.

Before your worries have time to take root, you do see her coming back, your little donkey.

And you see a man, the one they've spoken of, and he's riding on her. She's not for riding; no one has ever ridden her—she would carry goods, but she's not for riding.

Yet he is riding on her back; and there's a growing noise and excitement.

What's going on?

Lots of people seem to have appeared from nowhere, and many have taken off their cloaks and spread them in front of him. Others are tearing palm branches and spreading them. Amazing!

They come closer, and now the swelling crowds are chanting (rather like the Romans are supposed to do in the arena), chanting some ancient words.

"Blessed is the king," they shout. "Blessed is the King who comes in the name of the Lord."

"Hosanna to the Son of David!"

The son of David, you think. So he is a king! The King—the Christ of God. And he's riding on your donkey.

Feel the pride and joy swelling in your heart.

The children come and stand with you, silent with wonder. The king, the Lord, is riding our little donkey.

As he comes by you, he turns and looks straight at you.

In his eyes you see a "thank you," but you also see and receive a blessing.

You feel bathed in his blessing of love and grace.

You are filled with awe as the royal procession wends its way slowly up the road.

You bring the children with you and walk to the edge of the track so that you can see the procession.

It goes on toward the city; you watch each step, wondering, until at last they disappear through the gate.

With a sigh, you return home and go back to your work. You put away your tools, and sit down for the family meal.

It is a thoughtful meal, less chatter than usual, and the children keep asking, "What will happen to our donkey?"

Yes, you think, what will happen to our donkey?

Your night is restless. You sometimes feel pride and elation, sometimes a fear for your future—you cannot manage without a donkey, and you've only just started putting aside for the time when she's too old to work.

And you wonder what it was all about, and who Jesus really is—they say he is a king, the Messiah. You sensed his power, but is he the one who is to come, the expected Christ of God?

Sleep eludes you. You are up at first light and try to work away your anxieties in the patch behind the house, your head teeming with thoughts about the future.

Suddenly you hear the children shouting, "Come quickly; come quickly!"

You hurry around the house to the road, and to your great astonishment there are the two men back with your donkey! What joy!

But to your even greater astonishment there is a beautiful young foal with her.

"What is this!" you say, wondering. "Whose is this foal?"

"The Master sent a message to you," they say. "The message is this: 'Whatever you give to God is returned with a blessing.'"

The children are dancing with excitement. "What shall we call him? What shall we call him?" they say.

"That's easy," you say, "his name is 'Blessing.'"

And you remember—you will always remember—the blessing Jesus gave to you as he rode past on your donkey.

Debriefing/Reflection

Did you feel the reluctance of the market gardener to part with the donkey?

How has reluctance to give affected you? For example, giving something to a friend, giving money to charity, giving time to a person—especially to someone difficult; or giving precious time to a meeting or a church service.

What blessings have you received as a result of such giving?

19. ON TRIAL

MARK 14:53-72

On the night Jesus was betrayed and arrested, he was taken to the house of Caiaphas, the high priest. Late as it was, the whole Council assembled to try and find sufficient fault with Jesus to condemn him to death. They got people to act as witnesses and give false testimony against him. However, different witnesses gave different versions, and could not agree on the words Jesus had said. The Law was quite strict on this point: two witnesses must agree on precisely the words spoken. So the high priest and the others became very frustrated.

At last two witnesses came forward and claimed that Jesus said, "I will destroy this temple made with hands, and in three days I will build another not made with hands." The high priest challenged Jesus to respond to this, but Jesus remained silent. Eventually the high priest asked a direct question of Jesus, "Are you the Christ, the Son of the Blessed One?"

Jesus replied, "I am, and you will see the Son of Man seated at the right hand of Power."

Now to all these people, what Jesus said was blasphemy, especially as he had used one of God's titles for himself, the words "I am."

So the dramatic response of the high priest was to tear his clothes, saying, "We don't need any more witnesses; you have all heard his blasphemy. What is your decision?" And they all condemned him to death. Then they started to ill-treat him, blindfolding him, spitting at him, hitting him. And the guards, the temple police, took him and beat him.

Meanwhile, Peter was outside in the courtyard of the high priest's house, warming himself by the fire. When a servant girl spotted him, he denied having been with Jesus. Later she spoke to the other people around and said that he must be one of the followers of Jesus, and again he denied it.

Eventually one of the bystanders spoke and said, "Surely you are one of them; you're a Galilean," recognizing his regional accent. At that, Peter began to curse and swear, and said, "I don't know the man you are talking about."

At that moment the cock crowed and Peter remembered that Jesus had said to him, "Before the cock crows you will deny me three times." And he went out and wept bitterly.

Meditation

You are a follower of Jesus. Imagine you are one of the disciples of Jesus (other than Peter and John).

Your heart and mind are in turmoil because that evening Jesus, your beloved master, had been betrayed and arrested. You and the others all ran away when they came for him, so you are also feeling ashamed, and desperate to find out what is going on.

Imagine the feelings you have as you follow the people who are taking Jesus to the high priest's house to try him.

Now, thanks to John, you are going into the high priest's house, somehow milling along with the crowd.

Apart from the temple police who are guarding Jesus, there are officials of all kinds: chief priests, elders, scribes, the full Council. Waiting down in the courtyard are people who have been persuaded to act as witnesses, and who will be called up in turn.

You stay very close to John, and find your way to a corner of the room away from the lamps, staying in the shadows. To be recognized would mean punishment, perhaps death.

Fear is added to your anxiety for Jesus and your shame at having deserted him.

The proceedings are beginning. You can see Jesus standing between two temple guards. Someone calls for silence.

Caiaphas speaks: "Jesus bar-Joseph, you are accused of breaking the Law of Moses and of blasphemy. What do you have to say?"

You hold your breath, wondering how he will counter this unjust accusation.

Jesus is silent. He is standing calm and straight.

You think: perhaps this is how I must learn to cope with false accusers. You notice how composed and dignified he is.

Caiaphas looks annoyed. He clearly expects people to be subservient.

"Very well," he says, "we shall see what you have to say when you hear our witnesses against you."

"Bring in the first witnesses," says an official. Two men are brought in.

"What have you got to tell the court?" the official asks.

One witness says, "He said, 'Which is easier? To say your sins are forgiven; to to say get up and walk? But to show you the Son of Man has power . . .' "

Someone interrupts. "Did he call himself the Son of Man?" they ask.
"I don't think so," says the witness.
But then the second witness speaks up, "I think he did say he was the Son of Man."

There's confusion in the court, several people all talking at once. The high priest looks even more irritated.
You pray that in the confusion they won't be able to find a case against Jesus.

There's a pause. The high priest and one or two others are conferring. They look pleased with themselves.
You have a feeling of dread, wondering what they have hatched up.

Two more witnesses are wheeled in.
"I am a temple guard," the first says, "and I heard him say, 'I will destroy this temple and within three days build another one without any human aid.'"

There's a buzz of muttering in the room.
Your heart sinks. He did say something like that, but he didn't mean what they seem to be implying. Why are they doing this? you ask yourself; how can they think so ill of someone so good?

Jesus is still silent, dignified, and seems to rise above the unjust accusations.
They turn to the next witness. "Well, what did you hear him say?"
The man says, "I think he said, 'Destroy this temple made with hands and I will build another temple not made with hands.'"
The official questions him. "You think that's what he said? Can't you recollect exactly what he did say?"

The man looks confused. The previous witness starts speaking but then other officials start talking at the same time. There's uproar.
The high priest looks furious.
"Silence!" he shouts. The hubbub stops.

"Now," says the high priest, "let's settle this once and for all."
He turns to Jesus. "I'm going to ask you a direct question. If you remain silent we shall assume you are too guilty to answer."
The atmosphere is now tense and charged.
Imagine your feelings.
The high priest, in a commanding voice, puts his challenge:

"Are you the Christ, the Anointed One, the Son of the Most High?"
Silence. Dead silence.

Then Jesus speaks—dignified and in some way still in control of proceedings. "I am," he says.
There's a moment of disbelieving silence, then a collective gasp.
The high priest looks livid. And satisfied.
"I am," Jesus says and, speaking as though proclaiming a prophecy, he adds, "And you will see the Son of Man coming in power and glory."

Uproar. Everyone is shouting at once. You are petrified; Jesus has really done it now—claiming equality with God, taking the name of God for himself. You are very frightened for him.
The high priest is shouting, "Silence, silence!" and banging on the table.
The uproar subsides. "We need no more witnesses," he says. "He has blasphemed and condemned himself. What do you say?"
The council members all roar, "He is guilty. He must die."
You are devastated. This is the end for him. And the end of all your hopes. Your heart is leaden.

At that moment, one of the temple police passes close to you with a lantern. Your heart is in your mouth. Will he see you?
He stops right in front of you and there's a look of recognition in his eyes.
"I know you," he growls. "You're one of them, aren't you?"

What will you do? What is your immediate instinct?
Terrified of severe punishment, maybe death, will you say No?
Or will bravery or faith lead you to say Yes?

Whichever you said, Jesus now looks at you and catches your eye. He knows what is in your heart.
If you said No, his look contains love and forgiveness and understanding.
And if you said Yes, he looks on you with encouragement and trust.

You had to make the decision in an instant, with no foreknowledge, so Jesus is full of compassion and understanding.
You may like to reflect on the immediate reaction in your heart of hearts, and offer it to Jesus.

Debriefing/Reflection

Jesus handled the false accusations and attacks on his character with great calm and dignity. How can we imitate him?

Were you angry with the enemies of Jesus? How can we understand people who take up this kind of stance?

When you were faced with the challenge to say whether or not you were one of his followers, how did you react in your heart of hearts? What was your very first reaction?

There are all kinds of ways in which we deny Jesus: by accepting the values of the crowd, by going along with the pressures of the majority, by not always making it clear who we are and what we stand for.

What else?

And how can we do better?

20. Who Carries My Cross?

MARK 15:21-24

When they had tortured Jesus and found a way to get him legally killed, the Jews handed him over to the Romans to do the deed. The soldiers led the condemned men—Jesus and two others—out of the city to the killing fields. The victims were made to carry the heavy wooden cross-beam to which they would later be nailed. Presumably the soldiers wanted to get the job over and done with.

One of the prisoners, Jesus, was so beaten up and exhausted that he kept stumbling and falling down under the weight. So the soldiers picked on the biggest and strongest-looking man from the watching crowd, put the beam on his shoulders and made him carry it. He was a stranger to Jerusalem, having come a long way from North Africa. So it must have been quite an extraordinary experience for him.

Meditation

You are a young African man from the town of Cyrene. You are tall, and very strong.

Some time ago, you embraced the Jewish faith. Your adopted name is Simon. You worship the one God; you try to live a life in obedience to the moral laws of your faith.

However, keeping to the letter of the Law is proving too hard. Just as you think you are succeeding, you fall down again, and again.

How can you ever please the just and righteous God if you cannot achieve true obedience to his Law?

It has become a burden to you. You seem to be carrying its weight around more and more; the thought won't leave you alone.

Imagine the burden, the nagging worry.

How can I ever be right in the eyes of the Law? Fear eats into you. God is righteous and just, but he also judges.

Maybe the truth lies in Jerusalem, the spiritual heart of the faith. So with a group of your friends, you decide to set off and try to reach Jerusalem for the Passover Festival.

The journey is a delight; your companions are good fun, and you enjoy the freedom of the walking and rejoice in your strong physical well-being.

The only tinge of worry is—what will you find in Jerusalem? Will your problem be solved?

Be aware of the burden you carry, the secret longing to find an answer. How can any human achieve the level of holiness demanded by the Law, in order to be acceptable to the one God?

You arrive in good time for the Passover, and indulge in sight-seeing, admiring the temple, the great walls, and the fine palaces, and other buildings.

Then, the day before the Passover, you find yourself mixed up with a crowd on one of the roads leading out of the city. A packed crowd is moving in the same direction.

Then you see what they have all come to look at—three criminals condemned to death, driven up the road by Roman soldiers with whips.

Each is carrying a wooden beam, and—sickened—you realize that they are to be crucified, and these are the cross-beams to which they will be nailed.

The crowd jeers; but there are some women who are weeping for one of the men. You ask someone about it, and learn that he is a prophet called Jesus, who had claimed to be the promised Messiah.

Many had great hopes for him, a restored kingdom for Israel, a new hope for the faith. But he aroused the disapproval of the chief priests, and they have had him condemned.

As they come close, you see that this man is in a really bad way. There's blood across his back, where he's been flogged; there's a cruel circlet of spiky thorns pressed down on his head—his face covered in dirt and blood and sweat.

Then he stumbles and falls to the ground, struggles to get up but falls again.

The soldier curses him, hits him again to drive him on, but the sergeant shouts at him, "We haven't got all day. Get someone else to carry it."

The soldier looks around, and to your horror grabs you by your sleeve and hauls you out of the crowd (your size makes you an obvious target).

He's armed with whip and sword. You have no choice. You have a mixture of feelings; imagine what they are.

The weight of a wooden beam is nothing to you; you've carried one like it with sacks of corn tied on. You pick it up.

You get a big surprise. Two surprises. The beam is amazingly heavy—as though made of iron. You hoist it to your shoulders, staggering under its immense weight.

Then you get a glimpse—only a very fleeting glimpse—of the man's eyes.

They are dark and bloodshot, suffering; but in that split-second glance, you can see written in them . . . gratitude.

And also . . . love. Love!

Who is this? No ordinary man.

You looked into the eyes of someone who is exceptional.

So why are they doing this to him?

You follow the soldiers carrying the heavy cross-beam. Perhaps everything depends on this.

As you stagger on, the reason for its great weight comes to you—you have a sudden insight into what it means.

All your sins, all you have ever done wrong—lies, lust, greed, selfishness, anger, and the rest—they are all here in this beam. And your fear. No wonder it is such a burden.

Imagine how you feel.

Feel the weight of it bearing down on your shoulders. You must carry it, but you are bowed under and every muscle in your strong body is on fire.

Exhaustion sets in; you stagger again, your head is reeling.

You struggle on up the hill.

When you feel you can carry it no further, you arrive at the place of execution. The beam is taken from you.

You feel physical relief, but terrible fear for this man who seems so exceptional.

At that gruesome place of execution, they hammer great nails into the wrists and ankles of each man. The pain must be excruciating (judging by the screams of the other two), but this man prays to God: "Father, forgive them—they don't know what they're doing."

This is utterly amazing. How can someone ask forgiveness for such treatment?

You are still dazed with the effort and pain, but with the beam off your shoulders you feel lighter. And, strangely, you feel altogether lighter; a bigger burden has somehow been lifted from you.

Through the daze and confusion, you look on in horror at the execution.

But now, you begin to see what is really happening, another blazing insight—even more amazing than the last.

That cross to which Jesus is nailed contains not just your sins, but all the sins and evil that have ever been or will be.

All the violence and cruelty, all the hatred and greed and lust, and all the pain and sadness and suffering in the whole world for ever.

More. Although Jesus is nailed to the cross and hanging from it in pain, he is actually carrying, bearing that cross and all the combined weight of that sin and evil and suffering.

He, Jesus, is doing that for everybody—his enemies as well as his friends.

Surely only a man from God could do that.

You have the answer to your problem.

Jesus is bearing the burden of your sin and fear. God will now accept you as right and good.

And from time to time you will be privileged to bear a tiny part of his cross.

You decide to stay at the cross. You try to understand the terrible cost to Jesus.

You reflect on the impact of what Jesus is doing for you, and contemplate the love that can bear so great a weight of sorrow and affliction.

Debriefing/Reflection

Have you felt, like Simon, the impossibility of reaching the standard of righteousness which God seems to demand?

How do you feel about the insight of Jesus carrying your sins as well as all the world's evil on the cross?

Are you able to accept everything that Jesus is doing for you?

PART THREE

THE DEEPER RELATIONSHIP

You're with me in the quieter moments
With me showing me you care
Searching in the quieter moments
Your hand outstretched
Finds me there.
Loving me in the quieter moments
Brings surprise, surprise beyond compare
Finding in those quieter moments
A love that heals
A love so rare.

—Jo Williams

21. A More Excellent Way

Jesus was a traveler. He and his disciples went from town to town, village to village, staying where they could. Jesus made lots of good friends, and many of them looked after his needs as he traveled. Some put him up, some gave him meals, and some helped him to celebrate the great festivals.

He was on his way to Jerusalem when he came to a village, and was invited to stop with some friends for a meal and a chat. Now, of the two sisters who were looking after him, one was always busy and active. Martha was rushing around the kitchen preparing the food, peeling vegetables, slicing and dicing, tending to pots and pans. She was blowing the fire up, getting things from cupboards, putting out plates, rushing here and there, getting frantic and fretted.

And while she was doing all this, her sister Mary was just sitting. Sitting and listening to Jesus. That clearly didn't seem fair to Martha, who complained to Jesus. "Tell my sister to get off her backside and come and help me," she said to Jesus. "I'm doing all the work on my own, I need some help here. I'm frantic, I just can't cope." She was expecting, of course, that Jesus would send Mary into the kitchen post haste to do her share, pull her weight.

Not a bit of it. Martha got quite a surprise. Instead of saying, "Come on Mary, give her a hand, do your share," what Jesus actually said was, "Martha, stop fretting and fussing about so many things. There's only one thing you *really* need—which is what Mary has chosen; and that's not to be taken from her."

Meditation

You are going to put yourself into Martha's shoes. And those are your shoes and my shoes, but we shall be in our own time, and at one of our own activities.

In your mind, picture yourself at your very busiest. Think of a time when you have been really under pressure, with lots of demands made on you at once.

It may be in an office, at home, working for a volunteer organization or any other place where you have found yourself overwhelmed with the load of busyness.

Just picture yourself being very, very frantic and rushed off your feet. Feel the pressure, the demands made on you.

Imagine a multitude of tasks you are trying to do, like keeping so many balls in the air at once. And imagine the constant demands made on you, piling up.

You're really hectic, desperate in fact; it's all getting on top of you. The burden is getting worse and worse and you don't think you can cope any more.

There is someone who could help you—if only they would. (This may be a real person or someone imaginary—give them a name.)

They are not making a move to help you, wherever they are. You are aware that they are around, probably in another room.

If only they would get off their backside and lend a hand, do their share. It's so unfair.

As the work and pressure build, you can feel the resentment growing in you.

What they are doing is just sitting with Jesus and listening to him. There's a time and place for that, we'd all like to do it, but not now. They are needed here. Right now.

Feel the sense of unfairness.

Feel the frustration building, the anger.

You are doing all this work and they aren't lifting a finger to help.

And you want to tell Jesus just how unfair it feels to you, even how angry you feel.

So go ahead and tell him. Pour out your feelings. Tell it all to him, the burden, the pressures, the stress.

He will listen.

Be prepared for a surprise.

He doesn't tell the other person to come and help. He looks at you; he loves you. And he is very gentle.

He speaks: "There is something more important than all this rushing about. It is the role that Mary chose—to sit quietly, and to listen."

To sit quietly with Jesus . . . to sit and to be still, to listen.

So, prepare to change your activity.

Try to put aside all the tasks that fret you. Stack them away somewhere one by one. Put them in a heap in the corner.

Identify each task or burden, and deliberately put it on the heap. Notice how the heap stacks up.

Feel the load on your shoulders getting lighter each time you get rid of something.

When you have stacked up all the tasks, drop onto the heap anything that is worrying you.

Drop off everything you have on your mind: fears, anxieties, things waiting to be done, difficult things, puzzles, and problems.

Finally, when you have got rid of the whole lot, put onto the heap your resentment, all the feelings of unfairness, of anger, of being put upon.

Then feel yourself relaxing, becoming peaceful. Feel the tension easing from your shoulders. Sense a growing inner stillness; a feeling of peace is enfolding you.

And now—go to where he is, and sit down with Jesus. You can be totally still now, completely at peace.

Let yourself relax into his presence.

Stay still with him for as long as you feel able. No need for words. His peace is enough.

Simply be aware of his presence, his love, his joy, his peace.

Debriefing/Reflection

What did you put on the heap? And what *feelings* (for example, resentment) did you put on it?

How did things change for you as you set aside the burdens?

What happened when you went to sit at Jesus' feet?

We are only exceptionally called to a life of contemplation; usually we have to work as well as pray. But we do need to order our priorities, to give a place to prayer, and then to work as necessary. How can we do this?

In what ways can we change our lives—and our lifestyle—to respond to Jesus as Mary *and* as Martha?

What sort of prayer life does this encourage?

How can we reflect the silence and stillness of prayer in the turmoil of our everyday lives?

Can we find small spaces in our busy lives to give attention to God?

22. THE GOOD SHEPHERD

LUKE 2:8-20; JOHN 10:1-18

The life of a shepherd is rough and tough and calls for courage, loyalty, and watchfulness. He has to guard the sheep, especially at night, against wild animals. He puts the sheep into the safety of a temporary pen, or, in the fields near Bethlehem, into caves. Then the shepherd sleeps at the entrance to the pen or cave. Sleep is often disturbed, for he must be alert to anything unusual, ready to protect the flock.

Some shepherds out in the fields, not far from Bethlehem, looking after their sheep, were startled out of their wits when one night an angel of God appeared in glory. They were terrified.

But the angel calmed them. "Do not be afraid," the angel said, "I am bringing you news of great joy for all people. A child is born in the city of David, who is a Savior; he is the Messiah, the Lord. This is the sign for you to know him: you will find the child wrapped in bands of cloth and lying in a manger."

Then suddenly the angel was joined by a vast heavenly multitude, who were praising God and saying,

Glory to God in the highest heaven,
and on earth peace, goodwill among all people.

When the angels had left them, the shepherds decided they must go to Bethlehem. So they hurried there and found Mary and Joseph with their baby; the child was in a manger exactly as the angel had said. And they were so excited that they told other people before going back to the sheep, giving praise to God for the wonderful news.

Meditation

You are a shepherd with a home in Bethlehem. You lead your flock of sheep to pasture some way outside the city, moving on as they need fresh grass to eat.

At night you go to the caves, make a temporary pen, and lead the sheep into it for safety. Then you try to snatch a little sleep as best you can.

But animals prowl, and you have to sleep with one ear open. You feel safer when other shepherds are nearby, so you can help each other fend off wolves and other beasts.

So imagine yourself one night having led the sheep safely into the shelter of a cave, not far from the other four or five men who are also guarding their flocks.

The night is bright with stars and very cold, so you pull your cloak around you as you settle down for an uneasy sleep at the entrance.

You can hear the night noises of wild animals, some wolves, a jackal. Far enough away, but not as far as you would like.

You doze off eventually. You are dreaming—a dream you often have, in which you are counting the flock to check they are all there, but they are trotting around in circles, making it harder to count them. You try to concentrate.

Suddenly you are dazzled by the brightest light you have ever seen. You leap to you feet, terrified, shielding your eyes with your forearm.

A heavenly being, an angel, huge, blindingly bright, is standing there, towering above you and your fellow shepherds.

You cannot move. You can't run anywhere. Your heart is pounding.

"Do not be afraid," the angel says, "I bring you news of great joy from God for all people." You begin to feel reassured, but still wonder what this means.

"The Messiah, the Christ of God, has been born in Bethlehem, the city of David.

"There is a clear sign so that you will know that it is he. You will find him wrapped in bands of linen, and lying in a manger."

This is extraordinary. The Messiah is king, successor to David. The city is right but the manger—such poverty—seems quite wrong.

Before you can think this through, the dazzling angel is joined by a vast throng of heavenly beings. They seem to fill the world and the heavens— even more dazzling, if that were possible.

They certainly fill the world with glorious praise of God.

"Glory to God in the highest heaven," they sing. "Peace in all God's world and goodwill among all people."

You are overwhelmed by the beauty and glory of the song. It touches your deepest being and fills you with joy and wonder.

The echo of that glorious song will stay with you forever.

Then the shimmering heavenly host gives way to the dark background of the night, and the bright stars now look so pale.

You rub your eyes, wondering if it was all a dream. The other shepherds are converging on a small fire nearby, and you go over to join them.
They are very excited.
"Can this be true?" they are saying.
But you all shared the dazzling vision, so it must be true.

"Come on," you say. "We must go to Bethlehem and see this for ourselves."
"But the sheep," one of them interrupts. "We can't leave the sheep."
He's got a point. "Yet God has given us this wonderful message," says another. "We must be meant to go and see such a great event—the Messiah, longed for over so many, many years."
"Yes," you all say, "we must go and see Christ, the Lord."

You all agree that God means you to go, and that he will care for the sheep, and you hurry off for Bethlehem.
As you go, you try to make sense of the revelation.
How can God let the Messiah be born in poverty instead of a palace? Only the poorest would put a baby in a manger. It doesn't make sense.

You reach the city of Bethlehem; all is dark. But sure enough, there is a light. It's the stable alongside the inn.
That must be right, just as the angel said.
You gently open the stable door.

You are awestruck by what you see, a sight at once so simple yet so utterly beautiful that you feel God's glory is here as surely as it was in the praise of the heavenly host.
The stable is an oasis of joy and peace.
The father, Joseph, is at the back quieting the animals. Mary, the mother, young and bright, is sitting by the cattle trough. And there in the manger is the most wondrous baby, the Christ of God, God's miracle.
You kneel in adoration. The world stands still.

After quite a long time, you take your leave. But you don't go straight back to your flocks. You rouse the whole city.
People are amazed at the news. They come tumbling out of the inn, and out of the houses to see the Christ Child.
Eventually you and the others go back to find your flocks safe and sound. You give glory to God for this joyful night.

Then a terrible thing happens. The glory is shattered. Every baby boy in Bethlehem is murdered on Herod's orders.

You cannot believe that he can be so cruel, or that God could let the Christ Child die before he had fulfilled his destiny.

You are heartbroken. You mourn for many days and weeks. That short, sparkling moment of joy and peace has been destroyed by evil.

You carry the beauty and wonder with you in your heart always, but also the shadow of the appalling massacre, and a longing for what might have been, and a small tinge of hope that one day God will put it right again.

Years later, long after you have become too old for the rigors of shepherding, you hear amazing rumors.

One who claims to be the Son of God is preaching and teaching in Galilee and in Judea. What is more, he is healing sick people, giving sight to the blind and hearing to the deaf. And his name is Jesus.

Can this be the Messiah after all? Can the Christ be alive still?

You go into Jerusalem to see for yourself. And there he is in the temple precincts. You draw close to hear him.

There's some discussion going on with the Pharisees over the healing of a blind man on the Sabbath day.

You are amazed and overjoyed by what you hear. Jesus is taking the Pharisees to task for not fulfilling their role as shepherds of the people.

You know all about shepherding and how unreliable the hired ones can be, running away at the first sound of a wolf or a bear. And Jesus is using marvelous stories of shepherds and sheep.

"I am the good shepherd," he says. "The good shepherd lays down his life for the sheep, unlike the hireling."

You are thrilled and delighted. This is indeed the Messiah. He has survived Herod's murderers, and he is here, full of joy and love.

David was a shepherd king, and God in the psalms is addressed as the shepherd of Israel. It all fits together.

You reflect on the wonder of Jesus the good shepherd, the true and self-giving one from God.

The child you worshiped in Bethlehem is here and is good. He is more than good.

You go and talk to Jesus, and tell him your story—how you worshiped him when he was a baby, thought you had lost him, and have now found him again after many years of longing.

Picture yourself now with Jesus, telling him your story, opening your heart to him in the joy of finding him.
Picture his loving response as he blesses you.
Rest in the wonder and glory of his presence.

Debriefing/Reflection

You may at some time have experienced the loss of the brightness and joy of an early vision of Jesus; it happens to many on the Christian way. In what way have you been affected?

How have you nurtured hope in your heart and kept alive a flame of longing?

How can you find him again, more real, more strong, more loving, and more joyful?

In what way does the image of Jesus as the good shepherd help you? In the Greek, the word for "good" *(kalos)* means more than good: it means attractive, beautiful, honorable.

23. GRACE FROM LIVING WATERS

JOHN 4:6-26

In the middle of a hot day, as Jesus and his disciples were traveling through Samaria (the land between Judea and Galilee), they stopped by a well—a rather famous well known as Jacob's Well, because that was where Jacob had lived. The disciples went into the nearby town to get some food, while Jesus rested by the well.

A Samaritan woman came with her pitcher to draw water and, to her surprise, Jesus asked her for a drink. She commented on this: a Jew speaking to a woman, and a Samaritan woman at that.

However, Jesus said, "If you knew the gift of God, and who it was who asked you, you would have asked him, and he would have given you living water."

The woman joked, "You've no bucket, and the well is deep. Anyway, where do you get this living water? Our ancestor Jacob got plenty of water for his family and his flocks from this well."

Jesus explained, "This water won't stop you being thirsty again, but drink the water I give and you will never thirst again; it will become a spring of living water within you, bringing eternal life."

"Sir," she said, "let me have this water so that I won't be thirsty, and I won't have to keep coming to this well."

Jesus said, "Go and fetch your husband." But when she said that she had no husband, Jesus said, "How right you are; you've had five husbands, and the man you now have is not your husband."

She immediately recognized Jesus as a prophet and started discussing the true place to worship. Jesus explained that worship would be renewed, changed, no longer of the old order, but would be worship of the Father in spirit and in truth. "I know that the Messiah will come—the Christ," she said. "He will make all things clear."

Jesus said, "I am he, the one who speaks with you now."

When the disciples got back, she left her water jar and went back into town and told everyone that Jesus the Messiah was there at the Well of Jacob. And they all came out to see him, and believed.

Meditation

You are John, the beloved disciple of Jesus. It is a hot, sultry day, and you and the other disciples are tired and hungry as you travel through the land of the Samaritans.

Picture the scene, a short way outside a town, where there is a well. Around it are a few trees and shrubs, and well-worn pathways where people have come to fetch water and carry it back to their homes.

Feel the heat of the middle of the day.

Jesus is tired, and decides to rest at this place. So while Jesus sits down by the well where you have stopped, the rest of the group arrange to go into the nearby town for some food.

For some reason you too are feeling particularly weary, so you say you would like to rest while the others set out. You sit in the shade of a tall shrub a short way from the well, and rest.

Feel the bliss of taking the weight off your feet, and resting your back against the stem of the shrub.

You must have nodded off but, as you awake, still feeling drowsy, you are aware of voices. A conversation is going on between Jesus and a woman. You prick up your ears.

That's strange, you think; he is unconventional, but to talk to a woman, and a Samaritan woman at that, is extraordinary—not the way a strict Jew would usually behave.

The conversation you can hear develops on just those lines. Apparently Jesus has asked for a drink, and the woman comments on the fact that it is strange that he, a Jew, should be asking her, a Samaritan woman, for a drink.

Jesus now makes one of those statements which puzzle people and then set them thinking.

"If you knew the gift of God, and who it is who is asking, you would ask him and he would give you living water."

Now, you think, what can he possibly mean by that? How can water be living? He must be talking in picture language.

Before you have time to work it out, the woman comes back at him—she's quite a sharp one, but she hasn't got to the inner meaning of what Jesus is saying.

"Sir, you haven't got a bucket, and the well is deep. You can't possibly do better than our ancestor Jacob who gave us the well; there was always more than enough for him and his family and his flocks."

Jesus balances what he says with what she is saying; he has this way of pitching a discussion at just the right level, challenging but not overwhelming.

She is doing the same with her responses. He seems to respect her for that.

He counters her defense of the well: "When you drink water from this well, you'll become thirsty again, but those who drink the water I give will never be thirsty again. It will be like a spring inside them constantly bubbling up to eternal life."

You begin to understand; he's talking about the new kind of life, God-given life inside you.

But the woman still takes what he says quite literally, "Yes, please, I would like some of this water so that I won't be thirsty; then I won't have to keep coming back here to draw water and carry it home."

You smile at the way she's thinking. People so often get hold of quite the wrong idea when he's talking in images. But Jesus, as usual, has seen right inside her heart, and you sit up straight, listening for his response.

Jesus says, "Go and get your husband, and bring him back here."

That seems reasonable, you think, though Jesus doesn't usually ask people to go and get their spouse. He must have a good reason.

The woman replies, "I have no husband."

Well, you wonder, could Jesus have known that? If so, how could he be so tactless?

Again Jesus has seen inside her heart.

"You are right," he says. "You have had five husbands, and the man you are now living with is not your husband."

That's a bit tough, you can't help thinking that it's a rather destructive way to deal with the woman, whatever she has done. Jesus is usually more gentle with people in the wrong.

But the woman is not daunted. "Sir," she says, "I see you are a prophet."

In putting the challenge at precisely the right level, Jesus has done so with great love and care.

She goes on, "Our ancestors have always worshiped here on this mountain, but you Jews say that Jerusalem is the right place to worship."

You can see that she now perceives Jesus as a Jew with the insight of a prophet, and presumably a religious teacher, and that she is responding accordingly.

But Jesus leads her to greater understanding.

"The time is coming," he says, "when you will worship God neither on this mountain nor in Jerusalem. True worship of God will be spiritual, for God is Spirit, and seeks people who will worship him in spirit and in truth."

He seems to be encouraging her to make the connection between living water and the spiritual life that you have heard him speaking about before.

To your surprise, she not only makes that connection, but also the connection with the Messiah.

"I know that the Messiah, the Christ, is coming," she says. "He will make all things plain."

And Jesus makes himself plain. He says, "I am he, the one who is speaking to you."

You see an expression of enlightenment set her face aglow, as you marvel at this revelation.

At this moment the others get back, and start talking to Jesus.

You notice that the woman has left her precious water pot and gone; so she must have felt an urgency about fetching other people.

You sit back to reflect and think it all through. Living water—an inner spring of bubbling life—a kind of spiritual life—this is the gift and grace of God.

Feel the thirst for the living water that is Jesus.

Open your heart and mind to him as you sit with him at the well.

Debriefing/Reflection

What would Jesus say to you to challenge you, as he did with the woman?

Consider the words from Psalm 36: "For with you is the well of life, and in your light shall we see light."

What is Jesus saying to you at this time about your inner life?

How can the idea of a well of living water help you to understand and to develop your life in Christ?

How is he leading you to worship God in spirit and in truth?

24. YOU ARE THE CHRIST

MATTHEW 16:13-20; LUKE 4:16-22*a*

In the midst of a controversy with the Pharisees and Sadducees—the officials of the Jewish religion at the time of Jesus—the disciples and Jesus came to the far north of Galilee. They were in the region of a town called Caesarea Philippi, which Herod's son Philip had dedicated to Caesar, with his own name tacked on as well.

While they were there, Jesus put a question to his disciples: "Who do people say that the Son of Man is?" Jesus used the title "Son of Man" for himself; it has a wealth of meaning, such as the "representative" man who is to come in glory and reign over all.

The disciples were taken aback, but said, "Some say John the Baptist" (who, of course, had been killed by Herod), "but others say Elijah, and yet others say Jeremiah or one of the prophets."

"But who do you say that I am?" asked Jesus.

Simon spoke up: "You are the Christ, the Son of the living God."

And Jesus said, "Blessed are you Simon, son of Jonah. Flesh and blood has not revealed this to you but my Father in heaven. And I tell you, you are Peter" (thus giving him a new name, meaning "rock"), "and on this rock I will found my church."

Jesus said more about the role of Peter in his church, and then he told his disciples, very sternly, not to tell anyone he was the Christ.

Meditation

You are one of the quieter disciples, such as Philip or the other James. You are journeying with Jesus around the remote northern-most parts of Galilee.

Eventually you find yourselves near Caesarea Philippi. There, one of the main sources of the river Jordan pours out of a cave—a rushing, powerful torrent, endlessly fascinating in its powerful, driving energy.

As you stand and see the stream gushing out, you think that Jesus is like that. He seems to have a similar, continuous power—a miraculous, flowing power that never dries up—power to preach, to heal, to carry people with him.

He is life-giving in endless surprising ways, pouring out love and joy and compassion.

As you stand and reflect on this, Jesus gathers you all around him. You wonder what will be next, what new surprises, but you are quite unprepared for the question he asks.

"Tell me," he says, "what are people saying about me? Who do they say that I am, I the Son of Man?"

You are dumbstruck, especially as he uses that title again, "Son of Man," which, for you, means the kingly one who comes in glory.

Andrew speaks, "Some say you are John the Baptist."

You say to yourself, they can't be right; John saw himself as the forerunner and pointed to Jesus as the one to come.

James says, "Other people say you are Elijah, the prophet whom Malachi said God will send."

And then John says, "Yes, but yet other people say you must be Jeremiah, or one of the other prophets."

Well, you think, that doesn't seem to fit either. Jesus isn't like one of the old prophets. They condemned; Jesus breathes new life.

But then, what is he getting at? You know he is someone exceptional, and he must come from God.

Then Simon, the disciple who always jumps in, surprises you all.

"You are the Christ," he says, "the Son of the living God."

How can this be? you think. The Christ who is to come will be the anointed one, the King who follows David. Jesus is great, but he's no warrior king.

Jesus amazes you, as he so often does. "You are much blessed, Simon, son of John," he says. "This knowledge has not come to you from any human source, but from God himself, my heavenly Father.

"Now I give you a new name, Peter, the rock. I shall build my spiritual house on this rock."

You are astounded. Is Jesus really the Messiah, the Christ? And if he is, what has happened to all the old prophecies?

Then a picture comes into your mind. Jesus is standing in the synagogue. He reads from the scroll of the prophet Isaiah. It's one of the great prophecies about the coming of the Messiah.

"The Spirit of the Lord is upon me,
    because he has anointed me
        to bring good news to the poor.
He has sent me to proclaim release to the captives
    and recovery of sight to the blind,
        to let the oppressed go free,
    to proclaim the year of the Lord's favor." (Luke 4:18-19)

The atmosphere tingles as Jesus sits down after reading these words, with every pair of eyes in the place fixed on him.

Then he says, "Today this scripture has been fulfilled in your hearing."

And you reflect: this is exactly what Jesus has been doing since that day. He is preaching good news, news of the kingdom of God. He is giving sight to the blind in every possible sense; he has opened your eyes. He sets people free in all kinds of ways.

This is a wonderful new sort of Messiah. He is a revelation.

He brings vigorous, fresh, joyful new life to everyone who meets him.

Then you look back at that great torrent of water rushing out of the cave, which gives you such a lively image of Jesus—power, cleansing, fresh life, joy, overflowing love—all that is marvelous about Jesus.

As you reflect, you ask yourself: who is Jesus for me? How do I respond to his life-giving love?

Debriefing/Reflection

Who do people say that Jesus is in this day and age?

How can they, and we, be aware of who Jesus is?

How does the idea of the Christ, the anointed one of God, help us?

Does the powerful torrent of life-giving water give you a helpful image of Jesus? What other images do you find helpful?

25. SERVANT OF ALL

JOHN 13:1-17; MARK 10:35-45

At supper on the evening when he was betrayed and taken prisoner, Jesus surprised his disciples. During the meal, he took off his outer garment, put a towel around his waist and poured water into a basin. Then he went around the disciples washing their feet in the basin and drying them with the towel.

When he got to Simon Peter, Peter said to Jesus, "Lord, are you really going to wash my feet?" And Jesus said to him, "You won't understand now, but you will later."

Peter replied, "You shall never wash my feet."

Jesus said, "Unless I wash you, you aren't sharing in my life."

So Peter responded, "Then, Lord, don't just wash my feet, but my hands and my head too."

But Jesus said, "One who has bathed only needs to wash their feet to be clean."

Afterward he explained to his disciples what he had been doing. "You call me Teacher and Lord," he said, "and that is right, for so I am. So if I, your Lord and Teacher, have washed your feet, you should also wash one another's feet. I've set you an example for you to follow, so that you can do as I have done."

Meditation

Imagine you are one of Jesus' disciples. You are meeting for supper at a house very near Jerusalem. The week so far has been exciting and demanding. It began with a triumphant procession into Jerusalem, and has been filled with some high-powered teaching and preaching by Jesus.

Now you are gathered for a formal meal. Picture yourself with the others, seated around a table.

There is a festive atmosphere, but also a feeling that something very important is going to happen. Jesus has been dropping hints, which none of you has been able to understand.

So conversation is low-key, and when you have finished the first course, it halts completely. Jesus does something that at first strikes you as extraordinary.

He stands up and takes off his outer garment. You stare at him, wondering what he is about.

Next he picks up a towel and ties it around his waist. Then he pours water into a basin, picks up the basin, goes to Andrew, who's sitting nearest, and starts to wash his feet.

Andrew is looking a bit self-conscious; but he's an accepting sort of person, so he lets Jesus wash his feet.

You notice how Jesus gently bathes his feet encrusted with sand and grit, how thoughtfully he rinses the toes, and carefully dries his feet with the towel.

Nobody says a word. You are all trying to understand what he is telling you.

This seems to be not images in language, which he uses so often, but images in actions. You know he's making a point, if you could only work it out.

Next to Andrew are James and John. They both look somewhat abashed.

Suddenly you realize why, and a picture flashes into your mind. You see the two standing in front of Jesus to make a special request—a fairly formal and important one, it seems.

Jesus asks them what they want.

"When you come into the glory of your kingdom," they say, "we would like to sit one at your right hand and one at your left."

One or two of you start to mutter about this, but Jesus says, "You don't know what you're asking. Can you drink of the cup that I shall drink of, and share my baptism?"

This mystifies you, but—blustering a bit now—they answer, "Yes, we can."

They could not have known what they were saying, but Jesus responds, "Yes, you will drink of the same cup, but the places of honor are not mine to give."

The rest of you are furious by now. "Who do they think they are?" and "What makes them think they are so important?"

Peter is outraged, but before he explodes Jesus calms everyone down. "You know how important people like to lord it over others, and exercise their power. That may be their way, but if you want to be great you must become the servant of others.

"The Son of Man came not to be served but to serve, to be the servant of all, and to give his life as a ransom for many."

You are all stunned by this revelation, this upside down way of behaving.

Now you begin to see that Jesus is demonstrating this by washing your feet. He is your Lord, and is truly great, yet he is being a slave to you.

You see why James and John looked so abashed, though now, as Jesus dries John's feet, he looks calm and refreshed.

Next Jesus comes to Peter. And Peter is never one to let things just happen. "I'm not letting you wash my feet," he says, adamant.

But Jesus responds, "I need to wash your feet or you will not be truly in fellowship with me."

So Peter goes overboard. "Well, don't just wash my feet, wash my head and hands as well," he says.

"If you've bathed you only need to have your dusty feet washed," Jesus says.

So Peter submits with good grace, becomes calm and accepting.

Now it's your turn. Jesus, your Teacher, is kneeling at your feet.

How can this be? It feels completely and utterly wrong. I can't possibly let Jesus kneel and wash my feet. How can I?

Now you know why Peter felt as he did. It is so hard to accept service from someone else, especially when he is Jesus, your Lord and Master.

The experience is remarkable. Your feet, like the others', are caked with irritating grains of sand, but Jesus gently and smoothly washes away the dirt.

Your feet feel fresh and cool, but you have a sense of being soothed throughout your body and within your mind.

The cleansing embraces your whole being. A blissful peace envelops you, a sense of relief, of unburdening.

"You are to do the same for others," says Jesus. "I've given you an example; I, your Lord and Teacher, have knelt at your feet, my love has enfolded you.

"Now, whenever you give loving care to someone in need, remember you are giving that care to me—every act of thoughtfulness and kindness, a welcome to a stranger, a drink for the thirsty, a listening ear, a shoulder to cry on, a sharing of a burden—each is done for me.

"To become truly like me, you must become a servant to others."

You feel bathed in the refreshing love of Jesus; he has performed a wonderful service for you—which you know you must bring to others.

Debriefing/Reflection

How did you find the experience of Jesus washing your feet?

Are you able to accept God's love for you in Jesus? Are you able fully to accept God's free forgiveness?

Do you ever think of Jesus as a servant? You may like to look up Isaiah 52:13–53:12 and Philippians 2:5-8.

How easy is it to accept service and gifts from other people?

"The great power of prayer consists, not in asking, but in learning how to receive" (Marian Bushill, *Seed Thoughts for Daily Meditation,* The Guild of Health, 1986).

How have you experienced serving Jesus as you give love and care to others in need?

26. KING AND SACRIFICE

MARK 14:3-9; LUKE 7:36-50

Jesus was heading for Jerusalem, much to his disciples' dismay, and stopped outside the city at someone's house for a meal. While he was there, a woman who was a notorious prostitute (and therefore considered by the Jews a very serious sinner) came to him with an alabaster jar of very expensive ointment. She opened the jar and anointed his head with the ointment. She also knelt before him, weeping, and washing his feet with her tears, and then drying them with her hair.

Those present were utterly horrified. Not only was she a notorious sinner, but they also thought it was a great waste of expensive ointment, which could have been sold and the money given to the poor.

However, Jesus knowing what they were saying and thinking, put a question to Simon, the host.

"A creditor had two debtors," he said. "One owed five hundred and the other fifty. If he canceled the debt because neither could pay, who would be the more grateful?"

Of course, Simon had to answer that it would be the one who had been let off the greater debt. So Jesus pointed out that, while Simon had not given him water to wash his feet, or anointed his head, or given him the greeting kiss when he arrived (the signs of honor toward a guest), this woman had done all of these and more. She had also anointed him for his burial, although at the time they didn't understand this. In addition, her many sins had been forgiven, so she showed great love, like the one who had had a huge debt canceled.

Then Jesus said to the woman, "Your sins are forgiven." This made the people wonder who Jesus was, to be able to forgive sins, but Jesus added, "Go in peace, your faith has saved you."

Meditation

Imagine you are one of the disciples of Jesus. You have been invited with Jesus to a meal in the house of someone called Simon, who is a Pharisee.

Picture yourself around a table with other guests. People are fairly casual in the way they are seated, not with feet under the table but sitting sideways, perhaps leaning one elbow on the table.

The atmosphere is convivial and relaxed. Jesus is as prepared to enjoy good food and drink as he is to fast.

And he joins in the good humor, laughing and joking with the best of them.

Now something happens that shocks everyone around the table.

A woman comes into the room uninvited, but she is recognized as a known and notorious sinner, a prostitute. Such a person is thought by all present to be avoided as someone thoroughly tainted and untouchable.

You are frozen with horror as she walks up to Jesus. You now see that she is carrying something, holding it with great reverence, so that it looks like the most precious gift ever held.

A picture flashes through your mind of a priest bearing a sacred object.

Your curiosity is whetted as you peer to make out what it is.

Then you see it, the beautiful alabaster jar, the sort that is used for precious perfumes and ointments.

You, like everyone else, are now open-mouthed, still frozen, baffled by this intrusion.

You wonder, as doubtless the others do, how Jesus can let her near him. It is quite unthinkable for a devout Jew to allow this.

But she stops before Jesus and, taking the top off the jar, she anoints him, pouring the precious ointment over his head. The room is filled with the perfume.

In spite of your shock, a picture flashes into your mind: the ritual anointing of a king, of David, and of Solomon, and all the others.

Jesus is sitting, upright and dignified, even regal.

What will he do now? you think. And what will the woman do? Will she just go?

She doesn't go, but kneels at Jesus' feet, and you see that she is crying, bitterly.

Her copious tears are falling over his feet as though washing them. She then dries his feet with her long hair, and kisses them in a gesture of utter subjection.

The tension has broken now, and Simon and one or two others are muttering, "If he knew what sort of woman this is, he wouldn't let her near him."

What a waste! Such ointment could be sold and the money given to help poor people buy food."

Well, you have to admit, they have a point. You wonder what Jesus makes of it all.

Jesus as always is very aware of people's thoughts, and although he addresses his response to Simon you know it is meant for each of you.

"Simon," he says, "imagine a man who was owed money by two people; one owed five hundred pounds and the other fifty. Neither could possibly pay, so, feeling generous, he let them both off. Now, which is going to be more grateful?"

You all know the answer. "The one who was let off most."

Jesus says, "Now Simon, you didn't treat me like an honored guest when I arrived. But this woman, whom you revile, has done everything to honor me.

"She has anointed me with costly ointment. She has washed my feet, and kissed them. She is showing the greatest possible love because her many sins are forgiven. Remember the one who was forgiven most was the most grateful."

You have a sense of shame that you, like the others, had not seen what was really happening.

"This woman," Jesus continues, "has done a great service for me. She has done what was in her gift to do, she has anointed my body for burial."

So even more was happening than you had thought.

The others look baffled as well.

Jesus now turns to the woman. "Go in peace," he says, "your sins are forgiven."

Who is this who can forgive sins? Who can be anointed apparently as a King, yet foresee his own burial? Who is this man?

Your mind reels. Thoughts—scenes from his life—flash through your mind.

Some things begin to fall into place. Jesus is going to Jerusalem. He has been foretelling his death there, although this you can't understand.

You recall what Mary his mother had said about the mysterious visitors from the East who had come to pay homage after he was born.

You think of the symbolic presents they had given: gold and frankin-cense and myrrh. King and priest and sacrifice. Anointing and forgiveness.

You reflect on who Jesus is and the divine power he brings to the woman and to Simon and to you—forgiveness, remaking, kingly rule—all some-how connected with his death.

Now you feel that you have some partial understanding, and you pray to have more one day. But for the present, you can only rest in his love, his forgiving love, and contemplate the generosity of his goodness.

Debriefing/Reflection

What does this event tell you about forgiveness?

Do you feel able to accept free forgiveness from God? And how does that make you feel?

What new insights do you gain about the person of Jesus? His kingship, his understanding of his destiny, his sacrifice of himself, for example?

27. JESUS IS ALL

JOHN 19:25-30

When Jesus was so cruelly nailed to the cross, those closest to him were brave enough to be there, as witnesses, giving him their love and devotion, torn by grief yet never willing to leave him. These included Mary his mother (remembering Simeon's prophecy, "A sword will pierce your heart"), and John, the beloved disciple. Despite his agony of body and spirit, Jesus was able to say to his mother, "Mother, here is your son," meaning John; and to John, "This is your mother." And from then on, John took Mary into his home as an honored member of his family.

Meanwhile, they and others who loved Jesus stayed near the cross, watching and grieving.

Later, Jesus said, "I am thirsty," and they gave him a little wine. His final words were, "It is finished," meaning that he had completed his work in this world. And he bowed his head and died.

Meditation

You are Simon of Cyrene. Your shoulders and back and neck and arms are still aching and burning from carrying the crossbeam of Jesus' cross, the weight huge because, as you saw with sudden insight, all of our sins and failings and fears were contained in it.

Now you are altogether lightened from your life's burden, but you are faced with the hideous scene of execution.

Imagine your feelings.

Picture the scene: three men skewered to wooden crosses by cruel nails, their bodies streaked with blood and sweat and dirt, their faces contorted with pain; below, a crowd, some jeering and mocking, others grieving and heartbroken.

You are still dazed by the even more startling insight that Jesus on the cross is bearing the sins and pains and evils of the whole world for all time.

But you are also appalled by the terrible scene in front of you: the cruel and bloody crucifixion of three men.

You are horrified that Jesus, so good and loving, should be suffering this barbarous death. Yet somehow you feel strangely drawn to Jesus. In spite of the hideous situation, he still has the power to draw people to him.

And you wonder how that can be.

You decide to stay by the cross, for surely God is somewhere in this, lifting the burden of sin you have been carrying.

It's getting very dark as black thunderclouds cover the sun.

You find yourself next to a young man who is looking after a woman somewhat older. They look to be suffering the deepest possible grief.

The young man speaks to you. "Brother," he says, "thank you for carrying his cross. I don't think he could have gone any further."

You are touched, but carrying the cross was also a privilege. Now you are beginning to have a sense that you somehow belong to Jesus.

"I was forced into it," you reply, "but my eyes have been opened."

The sky is now almost totally black.

"My name is John," says the young man, "and this is Mary, his mother. I have been one of his close followers these last three years, and gradually my eyes too have been opened."

There's a rumble of thunder. You are still for a time.

John speaks again. "We, his followers, have come to love him and worship him. He has shown God's glory in his words and deeds.

"He is indeed the Son of God. Mary will tell you that before he was born, one of the names given to him was Immanuel, God with us."

You stand together in silence for a while, looking on, drawn together by mutual grief.

John seems to be trying to recall something. He is muttering to himself, "If I be lifted up . . ."

There's a powerful crash of thunder, but in any case Mary stops him from speaking.

"Listen," she says. "He is trying to say something."

None of you has taken your eyes off Jesus. You feel paralyzed by the horror.

Jesus is speaking, though it must be agony for him to raise himself on wrists and feet to draw enough breath.

"Mother, let this be your son," he says. He is committing John into Mary's care.

What can this mean? What compelling love is this?

But then he says more: "Brother John, here is your mother."

You look at her with wonder and respect; she has borne the Son of God, yet she has also borne all the agony of seeing him suffer. Your love for Jesus and his followers grows.

John tells Mary that from now on she shall have an honored place in his family.

Your attention is caught as Jesus speaks again.

"I am thirsty," he says.

If only you could do something for him. You long to respond to his love.

Someone puts a sponge soaked in wine onto the end of a cane, lifts it and holds it to his mouth, but it has hardly touched his lips when he gives a great shout—a shout of mingled pain and triumph.

"It is finished!"

Then his head falls forward and he dies.

It is an unbearable, terrible death. Is this completion? Fulfillment?

Or is it an abject failure?

There's a final thunderclap, then a profound silence.

You stand for a time, overwhelmed with emotion. Lost, torn, broken-hearted. Why this terrible end?

Imagine the feelings that engulf you.

What now? You would like to be a disciple of Jesus, like John, but how can you when he is dead?

You are wondering what to do next. Where do you go from here? Find your companions and head back to Cyrene?

You can't do that, for your world—perhaps everybody's world—has been changed beyond recognition.

Friday comes to an end. You go and hide away in your lodging, abandoning yourself to the sense of loss.

You felt your burden of sin lifted, but then there was the loss of Jesus.

Feel the mixture of release, for your burden of sin is lifted, and of desolation and loss, for Jesus is no more.

For the time being, you are just aimless.

Now it is Sunday midmorning. After two sleepless nights you feel you must move on. But where?

Suddenly John bursts into the place where you are staying.

"Thank God I've found you," he says. "Jesus is ALIVE! He is risen from the dead. It's not over, it's just beginning."

Your heart turns over. You want to leap for joy.

"It's true. We've seen him," John says. "He's been victorious after all, he's conquered death! He promised us and we didn't understand.

"Come and join us now—you may even see him alive! He promised us he would be with us till the end of the world."

You can hardly believe what is happening. You thought your world had changed; now a new life is truly beginning.

He has truly conquered death as well as sin.

Your joy knows no bounds—you are bursting with the wonder of it all.

Debriefing/Reflection

How have you felt the pain and loss and grief of the suffering and death of Jesus?

In what way can you sense that he is bearing the weight of sin and pain and suffering of the entire world for all time?

How can we in our lives share the joy of Jesus Christ raised from the dead through sharing his cross?

28. THE FIRST WITNESS

JOHN 20:1-17

Before the sun rose on the Sunday morning after Jesus had been killed, a great deal happened. First Mary Magdalene came to the tomb where he had been buried but, alarmed at seeing the great stone rolled away, she rushed off to tell Simon Peter and John. They in turn ran to the tomb and found it empty. John got there first, but did not go in. Peter arrived, went in, and saw that something miraculous had happened, and then John, too, went in. The body of Jesus had gone and just the grave-clothes were left lying. They didn't yet understand what had really happened, and went back home.

Mary stood outside weeping and, looking in the tomb, saw two angels, who asked why she was crying. "They have taken away my Lord," she said, "and I don't know where they have put him."

Then she turned around and saw Jesus standing there, but thought he was the gardener.

So she asked him, "If you have carried him away, please tell me where he is so that I may move him from there."

Jesus simply said her name, "Mary."

Mary instantly recognized him and exclaimed, "Master!"

"Don't hold me," said Jesus, "I am not yet ascended to the Father. But go and tell my brothers and sisters that I am ascending to our Father, our God."

So once again Mary rushed back to the disciples and told them that she had seen Jesus, and what he had said to her.

Meditation

You are the gardener of a very beautiful garden just on the edge of Jerusalem. Lovely things grow there: trees, shrubs, flowers, as well as herbs and spices.

It also happens that there is a tomb in the garden, carved out of an outcrop of rock. A wealthy Jew, one Joseph of Arimathea, owns the tomb, that had been intended for his own burial.

Picture this place. A tranquil garden, beautiful, peaceful; and the softly colored stone tomb like a monument watching over the place.

They are attractive surroundings in which to work, and it's satisfying work to tend such a fine garden.

You are in the garden in the early morning, about to start the day's labor.
Imagine the atmosphere of tranquillity, the soft sunlight filtering through the trees and shrubs, lighting the flowers and foliage.

Last Friday evening, however, the tranquillity had been disturbed.
Before you left work, some strange things had happened. Joseph had given away the tomb intended for himself.
He and another important person, Nicodemus, had overseen the burial of a man who had been executed as a criminal, although you believed he had been a good and holy man and a prophet of some note.
Certainly many had great hopes of him, and he had healed sick people.

You had heard some of his teaching. It made very good sense, although there was much you had not yet understood.
However, an upright teacher such as Jesus was surely to be respected.
So, it was sad that the officials had condemned him to death.

The burial, from what you could see, was that of a man of great honor, with a huge quantity of expensive spices. This had surprised you, after he had been executed as a criminal.

The Romans, in conjunction with the temple officials, had organized a guard for the tomb. They had the great stone rolled in front of the entrance.
You had been pushed out, told to go home early.

Now it is Sunday morning and you are getting ready for work after the Sabbath day rest.
It is a lovely fresh spring morning, hardly yet light; the best time of the day.
Feel the peace and freshness of this early morning, as you breathe the clean spring air. Picture again the beauty and tranquillity of the garden.

You begin to get yourself and your tools organized; you can just see the rock tomb through the leaves of a shrubbery.
Suddenly you notice with a start that the great stone has been moved.
That strikes you as very strange; surely the whole idea was to stop anyone raiding the tomb.

But the guards have gone too, so you cannot imagine what has happened.

You are still wondering what it all means when a man comes running to the tomb, closely followed by another. You think you recognize them both as followers of Jesus.

After them comes a woman, whom you also remember as a follower. They seem excited and perturbed.

The second man goes inside the tomb, and exclaims out loud, that the tomb is empty. Then the first man also looks in.

Whatever does this mean? you wonder. Has someone raided the tomb?

But surely not with the guards there.

The two men show surprise and concern. But they go rushing off again, talking excitedly.

Early morning peace returns. Or nearly; for now you are aware of someone crying bitterly near the tomb.

Peering through the shrubbery, you can see that it is the woman who came after the two men.

She's talking out loud through her tears, "They have taken away my Lord and I don't know where they have put him."

This man's followers had been very devoted to him; if the guards had still been here she would have risked punishment or worse.

You hear her speaking again to herself, still sobbing bitterly. "There's the gardener," she is saying. "Maybe he's moved him."

You are startled; surely she hasn't seen you through the foliage of the shrubs?

Then you realize she's seen another man and mistaken him for you. You move a bit so that you can see him properly.

A spine-tingling thrill—surely that's the man Jesus whom they buried. Now you are surprised and disquieted!

He was dead and buried. Very dead. How can this be?

You are astounded.

There's something very different about him too.

He's human all right, but also somehow more than human. Ethereal, yet very real.

She still thinks he's you. "Sir," she says, "if you have moved him, please tell me where so that I can take him away."

The man speaks one word: "Mary," just her name, but so personal and embracing—and alive.

She is suddenly on fire with joy—she's recognized him. "Master," she says, and she falls at his feet, holding them in adoration.

He speaks again. "You can't hold on to me at present," he says. "I am ascending to the Father, to your God and my God. Just go and tell my brothers and sisters, and be blessed in your going."

You reflect again: what does this mean? All sorts of things are being turned upside down. Death, even.

Mary is glowing as she turns to go, alight with his blessing.

He must be a marvelous and miraculous person.

You try to look again at him—but he is no longer there.

He may be human and he is surely of God, as he had said.

Now pieces of his teaching come back to you and begin to fall into place.

"I am the Way," he said, "I am Truth, I am Life."

You think about this.

You reflect on the meaning: following him as the way.

Believing in him as truth, and giver of life—true life.

"I am the vine and you are the branches."

He also talked about dying and rising again on the third day.

He has walked through death—defeated death.

There is new life in him, fed by him, like the branches of the vine.

Somehow we can now be part of his being, and his life can be in us. His life of love in us can grow and grow.

You find yourself overawed, overwhelmed with the wonder of it.

You can do nothing but contemplate such wondrous love.

Debriefing/Reflection

Can you share the sense of initial disbelief that then turns to recognition and joy on the part of Mary and the gardener?

In what ways do you experience the joy of Jesus risen from the dead, now alive and with us always?

How do we recognize the risen Christ? When and how does he meet us?

29. Our Hearts Burn Within Us

LUKE 24:13-33

While the disciples were still shattered by the death of Jesus, stories began to circulate suggesting that he might be alive after all. The city of Jerusalem was buzzing with such stories. However, while most people discounted them, the disciples found them disturbing. So when two of them set out for the village of Emmaus, a few miles from Jerusalem, they could talk of nothing else.

As they walked and talked, they were joined by a stranger—Jesus himself, but they did not recognize him. The stranger asked them what they were discussing so intensely. They were so surprised that he appeared to know nothing of the recent events that they stopped quite still. They looked sad, as they explained to him that he must be the only person in Jerusalem not to have heard what had happened in the last few days.

When he asked, "What things?" they set about explaining.

They told him about Jesus of Nazareth, a prophet mighty in deed and word before God and all the people, and how the chief priest and other leaders had handed him over to be condemned to death and crucified.

"We had hoped," they said, "that he would be the one who was going to restore Israel. Now it's the third day since this happened. Some women claimed this morning that his tomb is empty, and that they had had a vision of angels who said he is alive. Others who went to the tomb found it empty, but they did not see him."

"How foolish you are," said the stranger, "and how slow of heart to believe all that the prophets have declared. Was it not necessary that the Messiah should suffer before entering into his glory?"

Then he began interpreting the scriptures to them and all that was spoken concerning himself.

When they got to Emmaus, he made as if to go on, but they persuaded him to stay with them. When they sat down at the table for the meal, Jesus took the bread, blessed, and broke it, and gave it to them.

Then their eyes were opened and they recognized him. And he vanished from their sight. They said to each other, "Didn't our hearts burn within us while he opened the scriptures to us?"

Meditation

You are one of the wider circle of the followers of Jesus (not one of the twelve disciples). Like the others, you have been torn by the events of the last Friday; by the arrest, the false trial, and the crucifixion of Jesus.

You are grief-stricken at his death, and deeply disappointed; you had hoped that Jesus would set Israel free from the power of the Romans and restore the land once again to the independent kingdom that it used to be. Now, on Sunday afternoon, you and your friend Cleopas are walking to the village of Emmaus where he and his wife, Mary, live. They have invited you to go and stay with them.

You welcome the opportunity to walk, to leave behind the sadness of Jerusalem, the hopes now dashed and the loss of your great master and friend, Jesus.

As you walk, the burden of grief and blighted hope is with you still. You and Cleopas find yourselves discussing the events of these last days, for the hundredth time.

It's all the more disturbing because of the rumors going around.

The women had gone to the tomb and found it empty, but reported a vision of angels who said that Jesus was alive.

Peter and John had gone there too, and found the tomb empty, but no Jesus.

What can it all mean? you keep asking each other. There seems to be no sense in it.

Anyway, you both say, if Jesus really was the Messiah, why did he die? That wasn't the expectation at all. He was to be king and reign over a restored kingdom of Israel. He talked so much about his Kingdom.

Your conversation goes around in circles.

As you continue on your way, a stranger catches up with you and begins to walk with you.

You exchange greetings, and then he says, "What were you discussing so ardently just now?"

You explain that it was the events of the last three days in Jerusalem.

"What events?" he says.

You are dumbfounded and stop still in your tracks. Surely there can't be anyone who hasn't heard something of the goings-on?

You say so to him.

Then the sense of misery overwhelms you again. You feel utterly heart-broken that Jesus should have died, and died so cruelly and at such a time.

You can hardly speak, and Cleopas explains. "We were followers of Jesus of Nazareth," he says. "He was a truly great prophet, a powerful preacher, and he healed the sick, and did much good work."

"Yes," you add, "and we thought he was the Messiah, the Christ of God, come to set Israel free, and to restore the kingdom. Now we are devastated and utterly lost."

"You don't need to be down-hearted," says the stranger, "that's foolish of you. The Messiah had to suffer all those things before entering into his glory."

Now you are speechless again. What can he mean, "enter into his glory"?

How could Jesus, if he was the Messiah, possibly enter into glory now that he's dead?

The stranger says, "Let's consider the scriptures together, and perhaps you will understand."

He starts to talk about Moses. Then you are transfixed as he quotes the prophet Isaiah; you had never connected this with the Messiah before:

My servant . . . shall be exalted and lifted up, and shall be very high. (Isaiah 52:13)

He was wounded for our sins, and crushed for our iniquities;

Upon him was the punishment that made us whole. (Isaiah 53:5)

This is amazing, you think, Jesus the Messiah, on the cross bearing our sins and making us whole. Surely this is beyond belief?

Now, as he talks, the teaching of Jesus about himself comes back to you, and piece by piece falls into place.

"The Son of Man came not to be served but to serve, and give his life a ransom for many."

"I am the good shepherd. The good shepherd gives his life for the sheep."

Isaiah again: "All we like sheep have gone astray . . . and the Lord has laid on him the sins of us all."

So Jesus has become the ransom for our sins. New light is blazing in your mind.

"I am the light of the world," he had said.

"I am the resurrection and the life . . . whoever believes in me will never die." Another shaft of brilliant light.

Jesus could well have risen from the dead after all.

Maybe the story of the angels is true. Maybe this talk of Jesus giving new life, the living water of life, is true. Maybe we can share in this new life.
You have to pause and reflect on all of this.

You hadn't really understood at the time, but thought—you're ashamed to recall—that he was talking nonsense.
Now more of what Jesus had said comes back to you: that he must go to Jerusalem and undergo great suffering and be killed, and on the third day be raised.
None of you had understood it at the time.
So it could be true. There could be new life for you all. Your heart is on fire with the joy and excitement of his new light.

"For God so loved the world that he gave his only Son so that everyone who believes in him may not perish but may have eternal life."

To your surprise, you have reached Emmaus already, and the remarkable stranger is making as though he would walk further.
Cleopas attempts to dissuade him. "Please come and stay with us," he says, "Mary, my wife, will be glad to give you food and shelter. We would love to go on talking. Please stay."
The stranger is persuaded and you all go into the house. The meal is ready, and you very soon find yourself sitting at the table with the others.

You pause for the blessing of the meal. To your great surprise, it is the stranger who takes the loaf of bread.
You bow your head as the familiar words are spoken:
"Blessed are you, O Lord our God, King Eternal, who brings bread from the earth."
The words are familiar, but the voice—you know that voice.

You look up to watch him break the bread, and in a blinding, joyous, shattering flash of revelation you recognize him.
"It is the Lord," you say, turning to Cleopas, thrilled and delighted.
Then you look back at Jesus, and he is no longer there.
Cleopas too is ecstatic with joy and wonder. "Didn't our hearts just burn within us?" he says. "How could we not have known him?"

Joy takes over your hearts and minds—exultant, overwhelming joy.
The marvelous truth sinks in—Jesus alive and in the flesh. You must get back to the city and tell the others the news.

Now you are walking back to Jerusalem.

As you take each step, exulting in the utter bliss of knowing that Jesus is alive, sense him walking with you, alongside you, bringing you his glorious love and joy.

Debriefing/Reflection

How have you experienced Jesus revealing himself to you through the scriptures?

Can you sometimes sense that Jesus is walking with you?

How can we develop this sense, so that as we go through each day we are able to feel that he is with us?

One way of praying is to walk, and sense that Jesus is walking with you, so that you can talk to him, listen to him.

30. INTO GLORY—THE NEW REALITY

MATTHEW 17:1-8; LUKE 9:28-36

One day Jesus picked just three of his disciples, Peter, James, and John, and took them up a mountain to pray. While he was praying they somehow perceived him to be transfigured; his face was illuminated and his clothes appeared to be shining white. The disciples also saw two heroes from the Old Testament—Moses and Elijah.

Peter wanted to capture the vision forever by building three shelters for Jesus and Elijah and Moses. But at that moment a bright cloud overshadowed them and they heard a voice: "This is my Son, my Beloved; with him I am well pleased; listen to him." They fell to the ground in awe, but when Jesus came to them saying, "Do not be afraid," they stood up and saw no one except him.

So they went back down the mountain, not knowing at that time the significance of the experience. Jesus said to them, "Tell no one about the vision until after the Son of Man has been raised from the dead."

Meditation

You are James, disciple of Jesus. You have been with him some time now, and are at present in Galilee.

One morning, very early—before daylight—he calls you and two others, Peter and John. You understand that he is taking you up a mountain—not something you are used to, since so much of a fisherman's life is spent on level ground and on water.

You step out, the four of you, on a sort of footpath, winding upward. The morning is clear and fresh, and you find yourself reflecting on the time you have spent with Jesus over the last two or three years.

In the early days you were dazzled by the miracles, the many sick and maimed people he healed.

But you were also pulled up short by the things he said. He seemed to be teaching a kind of upside-down world. God's blessing was with the poor in spirit, he had said, but you had always thought the best of things came to the go-getters.

Love your enemies, do good to those who hate you. Difficult.

Slowly you and the others had learned his new way of being, of selfless giving, of love, and compassion. Rather like climbing this mountain. You feel you have moved on a long, long way. Jesus is bringing you to be more and more like him.

You pause to look at the sea of early morning mist lying below you, filling the valley, leveling out the valleys and hills.

Perhaps the prophets had foreseen this upside down world of Jesus. One of them had said, "Every valley shall be exalted, and every hill made low." The world of Jesus is new.

You clamber on up.

There had been all those stories he had told, wonderful stories with points as sharp as needles.

He had needled the officials too, the scribes and Pharisees for their hypocrisy. Old stories, sometimes, retold with a new twist—no wonder they were out to get him.

But you and the others had learned so much from the stories: the Samaritan who was a good neighbor; the simple sayings such as the wheat and tares growing together—God would do the sorting out in the end.

Then there were the lost sheep and the lost coin—God longs for and searches out his lost loved ones. He has found you and brought you home.

Ahead of you, Peter's feet are picking their way confidently over the rocks. Those feet had actually walked on water once, out on the lake. Then Peter had lost his nerve or his faith—or both. Jesus had been on hand as ever, and reached out to lift him up.

That's one of the great things about Jesus—he is there, sometimes unexpectedly, when you really need him, his hand outstretched for you.

You pause for rest. The sun is beginning to climb now and you can feel its heat as it lights up more distant places, towns and villages, hills, and broad plains.

On one of those he had fed a multitude of people. That's another thing about him; he feeds people—their minds and spirits. He even talks of living water quenching thirst forever; that is a spiritual gift which you will always be able to draw on.

Now you are high enough to see the Sea of Galilee, and you can see fishermen like ants coming in from a night's fishing, and spreading out their nets to dry.

That's where it had all started. He borrowed Simon's boat to talk to the people; then he got you to put out the nets, in spite of an unsuccessful night—not one fish. And then you'd caught heaps of fish.

That was when he had called you to follow him, along with the others. What a different sort of life it has been, new and alive.

You're very near the top now. Why does he want you to come up this mountain anyway? You can see the world spread out below like a map.

Was this the mountain he'd been taken to that time when he did battle with the Evil One in the wilderness? When the kingdoms of the world had been spread out before him? He'd told you what had happened.

He hints at a greater battle yet to come. When he has won that, who knows how he will change the world?

There's a flattish space at the top of the mountain. Jesus goes forward and kneels in prayer in the middle of it. You stand in silence.

Then it happens. Unexpectedly. The world changes, moves.

You will never be able to explain or put it into words, but in this moment you find yourselves outside time and space.

You have stepped through a doorway, it seems, into a different and miraculous world.

You are utterly dazed, blinded by the brilliant light. Jesus' face is shining, dazzling bright, and so are his clothes.

They're whiter and brighter than anything you've ever seen; the sunshine pales beside this light. You are overwhelmed with the glory. God's glory, surely.

You become aware of two people with Jesus—who is now standing.

With a gasp you realize that they are Moses and Elijah—those who had experienced visions of God in their lifetimes.

This must be the edge of the highest heaven. They too are dazzling in the splendor of radiant glory.

This is too much; you fall to the ground, overcome with awe and wonder.

In this intense moment you experience the utter holiness of Jesus, and you are aware that you are present at the center of all beauty and joy and goodness. And he is the center of all.

Peter is speaking, but he's not rational. He wants to fix this in time—something about shrines for each of them: Jesus, Moses, and Elijah.

But now there's a cloud over you, not a dark cloud but one brilliant with light. And a voice. A voice like the sound of many waters:
"This is my Son, my Beloved; in him I am well pleased. Listen to him."
There is a space of timeless, silent wonder.

You must have blacked out, because you remember nothing until Jesus' hand on your shoulder brings you to, and he tells you to stand up.
And you are back in the world as you know it.

What does it all mean? You hope that one day you may understand more, but you feel you have glimpsed a corner of a world beyond this world, and even in that small corner you have been transfixed with the glory.

You begin your journey down.
No words are spoken. You are basking in the joy and wonder of your experience.
Imagine yourself gradually descending the mountain.
You slowly take each step, and as you do so, each step brings you a sense or a picture of Christ in glory. You reflect on the wonder of Jesus.

Debriefing/Reflection

Were you able to experience a sense, however slight, of Jesus in glory?

How can we develop the prayer of wordless, silent space in which Jesus is present?

How will the vision of Jesus in glory affect your spiritual life?

WHERE DO WE GO FROM HERE?

Some Suggestions for Following the Way of Prayer

As you continue on your Christian journey, you will need sustenance, spiritual food. The chief source of such support is the Bible, where we find opportunities to meet with Jesus in prayer and thought. If you do not already use daily readings, such as those of the Revised Common Lectionary, then you may find such guidance a valuable source of support.

Your growth in the life of prayer may also be strengthened by the resources of those who have gone before, and have written in all kinds of illuminating ways out of their deep experience of prayer. These are valuable resources of inspiration and guidance, and many Christians find their prayer life greatly enriched through exploring these various ways of prayer.

There are many hundreds of books on prayer, and it may be difficult to find the right ones for you, so you need patience and a willingness to explore. God has a path that is his path for you, which will be different for each of us. The books mentioned here are only a few of the myriad resources available, but exploring even a few of them will help you to grow in the prayer of being in Christ and of Christ being in you.

There is one common factor in nearly all paths of prayer—the practice of stillness.

> We all learn to pray as we can and not as we cannot, but there is one aspect of the practice of private prayer that is universally valid and profitable, the practice of silence and centering the self. This is an intensely physical experience in which, by learning to still the body and hold ourselves in silence, we acquire peace in our own hearts. (Richard Holloway, *Dancing on the Edge,* Fount, an imprint of Harper Collins Publishers, London, 1997).

There are books *about* prayer, and books that consist mainly of *doing* prayer, but both lead you into prayer of your own. Among the books about prayer, a good place to start is *God of Surprises* by Gerard Hughes (Darton, Longman and Todd, London 1985). This opens up fresh thinking about God and about prayer. Another book to expand your horizons on prayer is *Jesus—Man of Prayer* by Margaret Magdalen (Eagle Publishing, Guildford, Surrey,

England, 1987), which brings insight, as the title implies, from the prayer life of Jesus in the New Testament. This book has a good list of references to other books on prayer.

There is great wisdom and loving inspiration on prayer to be found in a book by two authors from quite different traditions, brought together by their love of Jesus: Mother Teresa and Brother Roger, *Prayer—Seeking the Heart of God* (Fount, Harper Collins, London 1992).

Other authors who have written widely, and whose books are of exceptional value, are Thomas Merton and Henri Nouwen, both inspiring spiritual writers.

Books that lead you into *doing* prayer need to be taken at a gentle pace. In effect, you pray your way through them, allowing them to lead you into reflection or stillness. A good starting place would be a lovely little book on the prayer of silence: Jim Borst, *Coming to God—In the Stillness* (Eagle, Guildford, Surrey, England 1992).

A truly excellent book to lead you into prayer is: Margaret Silf, *Taste and See—Adventuring into Prayer* (Darton, Longman, and Todd, London, 1999). Gerard Hughes writes: "This is an excellent book on prayer and its relationship to every aspect of life . . . the author helps us glimpse God, seamlessly woven into earthy experience."

Marian Bushill was, on the surface, a rather ordinary person, a member of a large, Victorian family of Baptists. She was, however, a truly remarkable and gifted woman who overcame enormous difficulties. She has left us just one little book (still only 75 pages, but true gold), now published in several languages and in its 27th edition: Marian Bushill, *Seed Thoughts for Daily Meditation* (The Guild of Health, 1986). This booklet is best obtained by mail from The Guild of Health, Edward Wilson House, 26 Queen Anne Street, London W1M 9LB.

You will find references in a number of books to Ignatian spirituality, which is prayer and Christian relationship with Jesus based on the teaching and methods of Ignatius of Loyola (founder of the Society of Jesus, the Jesuits). This is a wonderfully rich and very practical source of prayer from which we can learn much to enhance our spiritual life, our relationship with God. An excellent introduction is: Margaret Hebblethwaite, *Way of St. Ignatius—Finding God in All Things* (Fount, Harper Collins, London, 1999). She says:

> Instead of propounding sublime ideals of what prayer is, so that you feel inadequate and do not know where to begin, Ignatian spirituality very practically

tells you what to do. And when you have done it, it tells you what to do next. And if the suggestion does not feel right, but something else does, then it tells you to follow the something else, because it is not Ignatius who is running your prayer life but God.

There are books which can be used for meditation in groups or by individuals. A marvelous spiritual writer is Anthony de Mello, who has drawn on Eastern methods of prayer to enhance the practice of Christian prayer. His best-known book, which has been translated into at least two dozen languages is: Anthony de Mello, *Sadhana—A Way to God* (Doubleday, an imprint of Transworld Publishers, London, 1984). Another very fine book takes the texts of a Bible-based retreat led by Anthony de Mello, and adapts and enlarges them: *Praying Body and Soul—Methods and Practices of Anthony de Mello,* adapted and enlarged by Gabriel Galache (The Columba Press, Dublin, Ireland 1997).

There is also a series of books published under the general title *Companions for the Journey.* Each book invites you to pray with one of the great spiritual masters, both old and new, and to share their journey. The publisher of the series is Saint Mary's Press (Christian Brothers Publications, Winona, Minnesota). They are widely available from Christian bookshops. The titles I have so far found particularly helpful are: Gloria Durka, *Praying with Hildegard of Bingen* (1991); Jacqueline Syrup Bergan and Marie Schwan, *Praying with Ignatius of Loyola* (1991); and Gloria Durka, *Praying with Julian of Norwich* (1989); but others among the eighteen or so titles will also be worth exploring.

Last, a marvelous book that seeks to help you to answer the central question which Jesus asks each of us: "And what about you, who do you say that I am?" This creative book helps us to construct our response from the Gospels, but also from our own experience: Peter Hannan, *Nine Portraits* (The Columba Press, Dublin, Ireland 1997). The book uses what are called the Divine Ideas of the Enneagram, which, Peter Hannan explains, "are nine aspects of reality as seen from a divine point of view. These nine ways of seeing reality are vitally important as they determine the way we feel and act and thus the way we conduct the main relationships of our lives." Each of the nine portraits, he says, "concentrates on one of the Divine Ideas and the way it helps us to gain a clearer picture of Jesus and of how he relates with us."

This is a book to come back to again and again, particularly for the way it helps us to discover our value to God in Jesus, and consistently reaffirms belief in that value.

Whatever pathway you are led to follow, God is generous in gifts and surprises. All prayer is his gift and his joy, and leads ultimately to his glory.

No words can describe, no book can explain what it means to love Jesus. We can only know it from personal experience. When he visits the heart, it is bathed in the light of truth. When his love burns within us, the world loses its attraction. Those who have tasted Jesus hunger for more. Those who have drunk of him are thirsty for more. But only those who love him are able to fulfil their desires—to know joy in his embrace now and glory later in his kingdom. (Jim Borst, *Coming to God*, 17)

232.9 Henstridge, John.
Hen
       Gospel images.